More ~~un~~solicited praise for
Turtles All The Way Down

"A literary masterpiece. Truly a hallmark of American ~~literature. And~~ *such a nice boy."*
— Gordon's mother

"Real Live Preacher was my constant companion through discernment to the priesthood and my seminary training. The writings contained in this book gave me an honest picture of the interior life of a clergy person while maintaining a profound sense of God's ability to work in and through all things for the redemption of God's children."
— The Rev. Jared C. Cramer

"Real Live Preacher is the only man who would get this Yankee to Texas."
— Larry Picard

"These essays will make you laugh, make you cry, and force you to rethink what you "know" about God and the church. your life may even be changed in the process. it don't get much better'n that."
— Dirk Bolle

"You need to buy this book. And then you need to find a place to read it all at one go because you won't be able to put it down."
— Stephanie Alford

"Fresh, Challenging and Irreverent. A modern dervish spinning in the complex space where faith and reason meet."
— Brian Hopper

"Reading Gordon's stuff is a light that shines on the murkiness of spirit work."
— Boyd Drake

"It's almost like a real book."
— Nathan Pruett

You're now allowed to
buy one of my books again.

Ever!

Turtles All The Way Down

TURTLES
ALL
THE
WAY
DOWN

Gordon Atkinson

Consafo Publications

San Antonio, New York, Cambridge, Brisbane, Ithaca, Creede, Cut and Shoot

Consafo Publications
15707 Knollpoint
San Antonio, Texas 78247
Consafo.com

Printed in the United States of America

1 3 6 10 15 21 28   e pie eye plus one equal zero

Library of Congress Cataloging-in-Publication Data
Atkinson, Gordon
Turtles all the Way Down / Gordon Atkinson
ISBN (10) 0-9788880-1-4
ISBN (13) 978-0-9788880-1-5
Library of Congress Control Number: 2009911763

Cover design by Mike Robertson
Turtle drawing by Shelby Atkinson

About Consafo

Consafo Publications is a community driven publishing company conceived and organized by Gordon and Jeanene Atkinson.

Consafo published *Turtles All The Way Down* as a community effort. Readers of Real Live Preacher bought advance copies of the book, providing the funding needed for the printing. They also voted on the content of the book. Mike Robertson did the cover and interior layout. My daughter Shelby drew the turtle for the cover. Fifteen readers of RLP with editorial experience volunteered to edit the essays. Kurt Norlin served as our senior editor and provided a style sheet and direction for the editorial team. Kurt was also instrumental in helping me keep the entire project organized and on track.

I wrote some stuff. My friends said they would help me get it organized and published. You know we did it because you're holding a copy in your hands right now. If you want another copy you'll have to go to my blog and buy it there, because I'm not sending copies to bookstores. Not that any have asked for it.

— Gordon Atkinson

Artwork and layout:

Mike Robertson—Cover and layout
Shelby Atkinson—Cover turtle art

Editorial staff:

Barbara Palmer—Editor
David Henson—Editor
Jessica Coles—Editor
Michéle Marr—Editor
Scott Eaton—Editor

Brad Whittington—Editor
Ellen Tucker—Editor
Jim Mann—Editor
Paula Jenkins—Editor
Simon Fraser—Editor

Brian Hopper—Editor
Janine Gastineau—Editor
Kurt Norlin—Editor
Sandra Silvera—Editor

The Consafo publication team:

Abby Nafziger, Achaessa S. James de Garibay, Adam Edwards, AJ Hawks, Alan Payne, Alice Tsoi, Allison Owen, Amy Forbus, Andrew Linscott, Andrew Prior, Andrew Tripp, Ann Voskamp, Anton Olsen, Aris, B. Gorinski, Bad Alice, Barbara Palmer, Betsy Grimm, Betty McDaniel, Bev Sharritt, Big Simon, Bill Finley, Bob Barrett, Boyd Drake, Brad Ward, Brad Whittington, Brandon Reeves, Brent Williams, Bret, Brian Hopper, Brooke Moore, Bryan Robertson, Carrie Mook Bridgman, Cassi Galt, Cathy/Chris Moore, Chris, Chris Beaven, Chris Enstad, Chris Martin, Cindy Long, Claud McHorse, Claudia Horak, Clint Porritt, Connie Hawley, Connor Carney, Cori Critch, Courtney Young, Cristopher Robinson, Cynthia Wilson, Dale Lewis, Daniel Whittington, Dave Hill, David, David Baker, David Hammond, David Henson, David Kite, David Liprini, David Spitko, David Tucker, David Tucker, Dawn Hansard, DE Adams, Debbie Brassfield, Debbie Foster, Dirk Bolle, Doug Mendum, Duncan Ballard, Elizabeth Cauthorn, Elizabeth Wallace, Ellen, Ellen Tucker, Elmer E. Ewing, Erika Gieschen Bertling, Esther Richards, Frank Vaughan, Fred Rogers, Giedra Campbell, Ginger Brandt, Gretchen Imbergamo, Heather Eaton, Heather Godsey, Hollie Atkinson, Holly Schubert, Ian Dunn, Jackie Rawson, Jaletta Parsley, James Gregg, James Noble, Janet Oberholtzer, Janine Gastineau, Jared Cramer, Jason Lehmann, Jason Moore, JD & Sara Whitlock, Jennifer Bentley, Jennifer Dyck, Jennifer Hamlin-Navias, Jennifer Trethewey, Jeremiah Andrews, Jessica Coles, Jessica Yusef, Jim Mann, Jo Bumbulis, JoAnna Miller, Joel Short, John Brewster, John Richards, John Whitmore, Jonathan Weech, Julie Albrecht, Julie Anna Sandidge, Justin, Kate Sterner, Kathryn Kieran, Katie Morgan, Keith Davis, Keith M Marzilli Ericson, Kelly Burkhart, Ken Nolen, Kester Wilkening, Kim Harris, Kimbrough Simmons, Kurt Norlin, Larry Picard, Larry Piper, Laurie Kehler, Leela Sinha, Leslie Westbrook, Lex Horton, Lisa Newton, Lisa Nichols Hickman, Liz Greene, Lonnie Massey, Lori James, Lorianne DiSabato, Luke McReynolds, Maida C H Vandendorpe, Marcus Goodyear, Mark Ashworth, Mark Childers, Mark Crenshaw, Mark Hobbs, Mark Powell, Mark Regan, Mary, Mary Latham, Mary Pleasants, Mary Salit, Matt Everitt, Matt Fry, Matt Grace, Matthew, Meguey, Melanie Stivers, Michael Bulger, Michael Kirlin, Michael Klees, Michael Poole, Michéle Marr, Mike Gribbin, Monica Cellio, Monica Enriquez Hedman, Nate Sara, Nathan Graham, Nathan Pruett, Neil Summers, Pat Hawn, Patrick Lam, Patrick Reeves, Paul Soupiset, Paul Walton, Paula Jenkins, Paula Tousignant, Penny Harper, Peter Yarde Martin, Petra Malleis-Sternberg, Phil Summers, Portico Presbyterian Church, Rachel Barenblat, Ralf Muhlberger, Reggie Freakin Regan, Rob Alderman, Rob Hardt, Rob Walker, Ronald Baldwin, Roy Goodwin, Royce Rose, Sarah Pressly-James, Savage Ink, Scott Eaton, Scott Johnsoh, Scott Kuykendall, Sean Dennison, Sean Roberds, Shannon Broyles, Sharon Guy, Shaun O'Reilly, Simon Faser, Stan Taylor, Stephanie Alford, Stephanie Woerner, Stephen Neill, Steve Friedrich, Steve Green, Steve Sims, Steve Winges, Sue Crannell, Sue Bethune Ristow, Susan Dipuma, Susie/Sam Drukman, Taryn Mattice, Terry Simmons, Theresa Coleman, Theresa Quintanilla, Tim Bishop, Tim Fairhead, Todd Wachob, Tom Cashman, Tracy Glaser, Tracy Rodarte, Trish Schmermund, Trish Ward, Victor Long, Vincent Baker, Wendy Bradley, Winjie Tang

For Jeanene and the three sisters.

With thanks to all my friends on the Consafo team.

Table of Contents

foreword to the foreword

Five seconds after I thought, "I guess someone should write a foreword," Keith Snyder popped into my head. And I knew with absolute certainty he was the right choice. The foreword he wrote is so interesting that I feel it deserves a foreword of its own. So here goes:

Back in 2008, Keith and his friend Larry came to our church for one of our wide open RLP Franciscan retreats. I say wide open because anyone could come, people of any faith or no faith at all.

Keith is one of those of no faith, an agnostic film maker and writer. Jeanene and I came to love him that weekend. He came to San Antonio and spent time with us on the retreat being silent, talking, listening, and singing. He played the water while his friend Larry sang an ancient African American spiritual that Sunday morning. Yes, played the water. He put a mike in a bucket and slapped the water to the rhythms of the song. The Spirit moved. People gasped for joy. It was beautiful.

And on the retreat, Keith received communion. Why? Because we offered it to everyone that weekend. Because it felt like the right thing to do with our new friends. And because I was thinking about this thing I once wrote called "Open Communion." So I offered and he received. He is not a Christian, but he practiced our faith with us that weekend.

Some Christians would say I was wrong for offering communion to unbelievers at the retreat. But in that moment, I believed we were right to do so.

The emotion behind that belief was so strong that I would have left the Church before I would have denied communion to the gentle pilgrims who were with us that weekend.

In all my years of ministry, offering communion to Keith after a weekend together may be the rightest thing I've ever done.

foreword

The oy gevalts ricochet down the halls of antiquity. My great-great-great-grandfather slaps his forehead and gives me such a look.

"Hey," I respond with a shrug. "What can I say, the guy's not full of dreck."

"Not full of dreck," says the patriarch. "Not full of dreck is a good thing. It's a mitzvah. But communion?"

"Yeah."

"Baptist communion?"

"Yeah."

"From some gonif in Texas?"

"A gonif in Israel would have been better?"

"Don't get smart."

"Look, who cares if I eat a cookie to honor my host?"

"It's not the cookie."

"Then what?"

"It's not the cookie."

"Well what, then? Tell me what. The cookie acquires evil powers in my digestive tract and takes over my soul? I thought we didn't believe in magic."

"I think you're a self-hating Jew."

"I think I'm a you-beating-in-an-argument Jew."

"You're funny, Who's this host with the Host?"

"You're funny-ish, but a little heavy on the Borscht Belt."

"Way after my time."

"Before mine."

"So nu, we're no Henny Youngmen. This host…"

"Uh. Yeah—I started wondering if I could find things to respect about religious people, even though I don't respect religions—"

"You mean Christian religions."

"Well…Christian's what I've had the most problems with, but—"

"I was right. You're a self-hating Jew."

"I'm a dead-altercockers-interrupted-by Jew—would you shut up?"

"This is how you talk to an ancestor?"

"This is how we talk to God. I should cut you some slack?"

"Tell your goyisher rebbe story."

"Somebody said I should read the man's blog—do you know what a blog is?"

"Do I know what a blog is… the big Jew from the coast asks me what a blog is…"

"Doesn't matter. Anyway, at this man's blog—"

"This Texasher shaygets' blog—"

"—there's no praising, no hallelujahs, no saviors. Maybe a little blessing this, blessing that, but he's a preacher, he's allowed. So he's writing about homosexuality, depression…but even if it's just the mouse turd on the communion table, or how he showed his little daughter the stars…keyword writing. He's not proselytizing the heathens, he's not grandstanding the spirit. He's dodging the easy stuff. You know the Mark Twain? The difference between the right word and the almost right word is the difference between a lightning bug and the lightning?

"Mark Twain, feh, it was Maimonides."

"Of course it was. Anyway, the lightning's there, and how often does somebody who's so agnostic that even the word 'agnostic' makes too many assumptions get to see anything from this point of view—let alone decide to fly out to San Antonio for a church retreat?"

"Why would such a person care to?"

I give him his own look. "You like everything in this world the way it is, or you want to maybe change a few things?"

"Change, what do you know from change? Nothing changes."

"Really? As to His essence, the only way to describe it is negatively. For instance, He is not physical, nor bound by time, nor subject to change. Sounds to me like the only thing that doesn't change is God—and that was Maimonides."

"You're not even bar mitzvahed. That was Google."

"Whatever. I went forty years without communion. So why all of a sudden?"

"You tell me."

"It felt like a good idea."

My great-great-great grandfather purses his lips.

"A literate, profane Texas Baptist preacher who loves physics and knows how to say he doesn't know stuff." I shrug as Semitically as possible. "I dunno— maybe you already got a minyan of those. But you're in the man's foreword, so you might as well read a little."

"In the foreword, how can I be in the foreword, I don't exist."

"You're a composite."

"I'm a caricature."

"We're all caricatures. In the great cosmic doodle pad of—"

"All right!" he says. "All right! I'll read the book!"

"Thank you for your blessing," I say. "So read."

— Keith Snyder

preface

These essays and stories were published between 2004 and 2008 on my blog, Real Live Preacher. I have written close to a million words there since 2002. My blog contains everything from my serious writing to offhand comments about everyday life. I am a writer who does his work in the world of blogs. A blog is an interesting medium for writing. With no editing and frequent posting, the traditional barrier between writer and readers has been torn down and replaced with something more transparent and flimsy. I frequently go places and meet people who know more about my writing than I do. And they often know more about me than I suspect. When you write with honesty you reveal more than you intend. I trust my readers with that knowledge.

Thank you for reading my words. And if my words have meant something to you, that is the most gratifying thing of all.

— Gordon

all that has ever been hoped

I will never know exactly what Jesus said, how he said whatever he did say, or what he meant when he said whatever he said in whatever way he said it.

You see my problem.

What I have are the tattered words, songs, and gospel remnants from twenty centuries of people jumping two-footed into hope. That's all I have, and I am keenly interested in these things.

I'm like a rag picker, rummaging through a mountain of moldy prayer books, old hymnals, triptych art, candle stubs, ancient texts, and other religious remnants. I crawl all over the pile, poking here and there with a stick. When I find something that interests me, I stop and take a closer look. I flip through the pages. I look at the pictures from every angle. Sometimes I tilt my head to the right, like a dog that has just heard something very interesting.

My friend watches me, fascinated. "Why do you seek the living among the dead?" he asks with the purest heart in the world.

His question stops me, and I look him right in the eye.

This is THE question, of course. It is the only question; it is the beginning of ALL questions.

Where exactly will you look for your answers? Why follow the yellow brick road unless you hope to see the Wizard?

I do not have an answer for him. I'm not sure what draws me to old books and ancient voices.

Later we're sitting together in a booth at a diner drinking Diet Cokes. He's working on the New York Times Crossword Puzzle while I look over my latest finds: a 1920 edition of *The Meaning of Prayer* by Harry Emerson Fosdick, a pre-World War II *BBC Hymn Book* with its stately, formal language, *The Way of a Pilgrim* and a beautiful leather-bound copy of *The Journal of John Woolman*.

I'm flipping through the Woolman when I speak without looking up: "I have an answer to your question."

My friend is delighted and immediately slides the crossword puzzle to one side. He puts his elbows on the table and leans forward, giving me his full attention.

"I'm searching through all that has ever been hoped, in praise of what can never be known."

He thinks for a moment, sucking on his straw until the loud slurpy sound comes at the end. We love each other. We both know this. It doesn't need to be said.

"That's cool. It sounds like a lot of work, though. Will you have time to talk to me when you're on break?"

This cracks me up. Then he starts laughing. Laughter begets laughter until we are out of control. It's hard to say what we are laughing at. Just everything, I think. I don't really care. It's just so much fun.

Between giggles, I manage to say, "You dumbass!"

But this only makes us laugh harder.

on a wing and a prayer

The Sombrero Galaxy lies 50 million light years away from us in the Virgo cluster and contains an estimated 800 billion suns. Someone named it after a Mexican hat, an act so incongruous as to border on blasphemy, to my way of thinking. Why not follow that by drawing Kilroy on a Torah scroll? Let him hang over the very name of God with his nose dangling between the He and the Wa.

I prefer the simple dignity of the Messier designation – M104. Whisper it if you must say it out loud, then let an astronomer/priest write it on vellum and slip it reverently into a wooden map drawer in some secret location.

One day I showed my oldest daughter a picture of M104, and we talked about 50 million light years. I say we talked about it, but that's not exactly true. You can't talk about something that is beyond the human capacity of understanding. I can't grasp the size of Texas. What am I going to say about a light year?

"There are something like 800 billion suns in this galaxy," I said. "And there are billions of galaxies like this in our universe."

We sat in stupefied silence, shaking our heads.

"Do you think there's intelligent life out there?" she asked.

"I do. Yes."

"How do you know?"

"I DON'T know. But I THINK so. When I consider what I can grasp about the size of the Universe, which isn't much, it just makes sense to me that there is intelligent life out there. Of course, we're pretty cut off by the limitations imposed by the speed of light."

"What do you mean?"

"Well, by the time we see or hear anything from distant star systems, the light or the radio waves are already millions of years old in some cases. There's a lot going on out there, but we can't see it or hear it."

She seemed very disappointed, so I told her about Voyager.

In 1977 NASA launched two identical Voyager spacecraft. Their mission was to travel straight through our solar system, radioing information back along the way, moving beyond Pluto and out into deep space. Radio signals and information will continue to be received from Voyager until its systems fail sometime around 2020.

After that it will continue to travel in silence for what we might as well call forever.

But Voyager carries something more than scientific instruments. It also contains a golden disc that was the brainchild of Dr. Carl Sagan, then professor of astronomy and space sciences at Cornell University.

This golden disc contains a delightful collection of sounds and images from our planet, as well as some mathematical symbols and keys to help an intelligent species understand it.

The odds against any intelligent being ever viewing this disc are, literally, astronomical. You'd have a better chance of finding a contact lens in the Pacific Ocean. The institute for the Search for Extraterrestrial Intelligence estimates that it will be 750,000 years before Voyager passes by another star system.

And yet, Dr. Sagan and others spent the time, effort, and money needed to create their golden disc. Why would they do that? Dr. Sagan said, "The launching of this bottle into the cosmic ocean says something very hopeful about life on this planet."

Indeed. I say it took great faith, hope, and love to launch this golden disc into the Cosmos on a wing and a prayer. The possibility of finding intelligent life was worth the effort whatever the odds.

I call it an act of pure worship.

When the end you seek is so wonderful, so unthinkably good, and so compelling that you would throw yourself against time, space, and even reality for the slightest chance of finding it, you are worshipping indeed.

And that is why I bow my head in prayer every day of my life.

my little girl is a laughing thing

My little girl is a laughing thing. A spindly-legged, curled in my arms, look at me, I'm naked thing. A tickle in the morning, blow on her tummy, bounce out of bed thing. A hands on, no fear, her body is my body thing.

My middle girl is a blossoming thing. A budding, elbows and knees, horses and rainbows thing. A lie on the bed, kiss on the cheek, tickle, but be careful thing. A hugging, sacred, her body is her own thing.

My oldest girl is a womanly thing. A breasted, sexual, hidden thing. A stare at the bed, sit on the edge and shake gently thing. A hands off, fear this, I know nothing of her body thing.

And I, it seems, am a watching thing. A stand on the platform, waving thing. A smelling the smoke, seeing the cars, afraid of the caboose thing.

A sad and lonely, smiling and fading thing.

all the right questions

A church man came to see me the other day. A churchy man, an important man in his church. A deacon I think, maybe. He came to see me and our little church. He came to see if there was anything of interest going on here.

I was wearing jeans and a Snoopy t-shirt at church that day, which put him off a bit, but the real surprise came when he found that I couldn't answer any of his questions.

"How many members do you have?"

"I don't know."

My answer, or lack of an answer, stunned him. He squinted a moment, trying to understand a thing that seemed impossible. It just isn't possible that a pastor could not know how many members are in his church.

"You don't know?"

"No. I could print a directory and count the people, I guess. But there never seems to be an occasion when we need to know how many members we have. So I never get around to counting them."

"Huh!" He frowned in an exaggerated way and nodded his head slowly and deliberately. This is one way that men tell you they don't agree with you but are going to be polite and not argue the fact.

"What are you running on Sundays?"

This is the way church people ask about worship attendance. The number they are looking for is a weekly average.

"I don't know."

"Really?"

Yeah. I mean, someone would have to count everyone each Sunday and run the numbers and all that. Again, there just doesn't seem to be any reason to do it, so we don't.

I wanted to be helpful, so I said, "Sometimes this room is pretty full. Then other times I notice it's not as full. And then sometimes it's sorta empty, you know, on a slow Sunday."

Turtles All The Way Down

I can't believe he kept asking questions, but he did.

"How many are enrolled in Sunday School?"

I was feeling a little sheepish, for some reason, though I have no intention of keeping these statistics.

"Yeaaahh," I said, dragging it out. The thing is, we don't enroll people in Bible study. We study the Bible, of course. People are free to join us if they like, but we don't keep track of it.

I could tell by his face that he thought we ran a pretty sloppy operation at our church. If you really cared about doing the work of the Lord in this world, wouldn't you count members and track attendance like any good business?

I got one final question, one last chance to redeem myself.

"Do you have a ministry plan of some kind?"

He didn't say, "Do you AT LEAST have a ministry plan of some kind," but I assure you the tone of his voice made his meaning clear.

"Ministry plan?" I racked my brain trying to think of what that might be. It sounded to me like some kind of marketing plan or strategy. "Well, you know, not formally, as such. I guess we would say that our plan is to do what's right, no matter what the consequences. We should do what we feel is right and good, whether it brings five people or five-thousand people to our door."

And that pretty much wrapped up the interview. He was polite and shook my hand before he left.

It's a very important spiritual discipline for me to let people like this think that I am an incompetent fool. It is critically important that I not explain myself to them. I just wave bye-bye and let them go.

In my defense, I can answer a lot of questions about my church. He just wasn't asking the right ones.

I can tell you anything you'd like to know about our children. I can tell you that Adam loves race cars and Steven likes to sing. I can tell you that Madeline's hair always smells good on Wednesday nights, and that Anna's mother is teaching her ballet. I can tell you that Jacob likes to be picked up, but don't turn him upside down. That scares him.

I can tell you about all the secret places at the church. I'm the one who cut the trail through the woods to the giant cedar tree, and I can tell you about the mysterious pile of rocks at the back of the property. I can tell you the funny story behind the decaying mound of wood and cactus that we call "Main's Folly," and

I know what the old ring of stones in the clearing was for.

I know why there's a rock in the back wall of the church with George's name written on it. I could tell you that story if you had the time.

I can tell you how the building looks in the moonlight just before dawn on a cold Sunday morning. I can tell you why Claud seems sad and why Chloe needs a hug every Sunday. I can tell you what Savannah means when she taps her cheeks, and I can tell you not to worry about what Lyle says because he has a heart of gold. I can tell you how Michael became a deacon and why Mark doesn't want to teach Sunday School anymore.

I can tell you about all of these things and more. I could talk for hours about the precious gathering of friends that we call church.

I just can't tell you any of the things that most people want to know.

the truth about snow

When Lillian was five she didn't believe in snow. She didn't say anything, of course, but I began to suspect my youngest daughter was an unbeliever because she talked about snow in the same way she talked about Fairies and Unicorns and Sponge Bob.

I knew I would have to be a little sneaky to find out the truth. I put her on my lap and looked right in her eyes. She looked back at me through her little bifocals.

"Lillian, are puppy dogs real?"

"Yes."

"How about elves? Are they real?"

"No."

"Fairies?"

"No."

"Goblins?"

"No."

"Cookies?"

"Yes."

"Okay, what about snow? Is snow real?"

"No."

I was right. She didn't believe in snow

It's not hard to understand how this happened. The last time it snowed in San Antonio was about ten years before she was born. Everything Lillian knew about snow she learned from animated Christmas specials. In her mind snow was like Charlie Brown, Rudolph, and elves with little pointy shoes. Snow was just another Christmas thing we wish was true but isn't.

Small children are so busy cramming all the new things they experience into their very limited set of categories that they really don't have time to worry about clerical errors. With scores of new ideas pouring in every day, they just file them as quickly as possible. Later, when the incoming ideas have slowed to reasonable pace, there's time to organize and do a better job of sorting things out.

I think Lillian was overcome by the flood of exciting images at Christmastime and simply filed snow in her "Imaginary Christmas Stuff" drawer by mistake. It happens.

I decided to tell her the truth about snow.

I have a way of talking to my children when I'm not kidding around. I use serious body language and a certain tone of voice that they recognize. Children are very good at interpreting body language and tone. It's the first survival skill they must master.

"Snow is real," I said. "It just never snows here because it's too hot. But there are lots of places in the world where it snows every winter."

I told her about the places where kids have heavy coats and yes, even mittens. It turns out she didn't believe in mittens either. I explained how kids make snowmen and build snow forts, and how they throw snowballs at each other. And I told her about skating on frozen ponds and making snow angels. I told her everything I knew about snow.

"Yes Lillian, snow is for real. It really, really is."

While I was telling her these wonderful things, her mouth slowly opened, and she shook her head back and forth like a person saying, "No." It's as if something deep inside her still couldn't believe that such a wonderful, fairy tale thing as snow could really exist in this world where most of the good stuff turns out to be make-believe. She trusted me, but her body revealed the conflict inside, as our bodies often do.

Then she believed. She put snow into her "Real Stuff" drawer and gave herself over to joy. She squealed and ran giggling around the living room with her arms out like an airplane, tilting them as she banked left around the end of the couch.

Her oldest sister came into the room just then. She was thirteen and entering the stage where she didn't want to appear excited about anything.

"What's up with her?"

"Oh, she just found out that snow is real."

"You mean she thought it wasn't real?"

"Yeah, isn't that funny? She thought it was like, you know, Christmas elves and all that. But I told her it was real, and she's kinda happy about it, as you can see."

Turtles All The Way Down

We watched her make a third circle around the couch, then tilt to the right to fly around a chair.

"And she believed you when you told her? She just believed you?"

"Sure. You know I always tell the truth about stuff like this, about what is real and what isn't in this world."

She stared at me very thoughtfully. I know she was remembering the conversation we had a few months before when she asked me if God was real. She had been wondering about God. She was wondering if she might have filed God in the wrong drawer. Maybe God belonged in the drawer with Santa. She wanted very much to believe in God, but she didn't want to be a fool.

She had asked, and I had answered. I looked her right in the eye and used my very serious, no-nonsense voice. I told her the truth.

No one knows for sure if God exists. Sometimes I wish we COULD know for sure, but it's one of those things that cannot be known in the same way we know that zebras exist.

That's okay though, because whether or not God exists is not the most important question. What's really important is how you choose to live. You may choose to believe in God and live accordingly, meaning you follow your best understanding of God's laws. Or you may choose to believe that there is no God. In that case you'll find other ways of knowing how you should live. The important thing I want you to know is that the ancient, Biblical idea of belief describes more than what a person thinks. Belief also involves decisions you make about how you will live and what authority you will follow.

I'll put it another way: A person might not know if God exists. But if that person lives as though God exists, worshipping and seeking and following God's law, then I think that person can rightly claim that she believes in God.

I know she was remembering that conversation. She stared at me for a few seconds while Lillian pretended to make a snow angel on the carpet. Then she gave me a respectful nod. Do not underestimate that. Getting a respectful nod from a teenager is huge. She knows.

She knows I will always tell her the truth about stuff like this.

apparently i might be
a false prophet

Someone sent me an email and told me that I am a false prophet.

I know! I was as surprised as anyone to hear it. At first I ignored the email, but now I'm starting to think. I'm wondering if I AM a false prophet.

I know many of you are not particularly religious and are wondering what I'm talking about. You're not exactly sure what a false prophet is, but you've probably picked up on the idea that being one is not a good thing.

You see, back in the Bible days there were men and women who spoke for God. They were called prophets, and the Bible is jam-packed with stories about them. It would have been nice if God had just spoken for himself or herself, but that's not the way it worked. In the Bible stories, God generally used people to spread the news, be it good or bad. Apparently this was some kind of team-building exercise for humanity.

The tricky thing was trying to figure out who was really speaking for God and who was a false prophet. And it didn't help matters that false prophets were often slick and confident and smart and that they said exactly the sort of things that everyone wanted to hear. Real prophets, on the other hand, tended to be rather anti-social characters who said things that no one wanted to hear.

All of this led to quite a bit of confusion and irritation through the years as people tried to figure out who was and who was not speaking for God. In recent centuries, hoping to avoid a lot of the messiness, some Christians have been saying that God only speaks through the Bible nowadays.

But of course, the Bible is an extraordinarily long and difficult collection of books to read, and most of the people who jump right into it with no help only end up more confused than ever. And right away they start looking for a prophetic-type person to tell them what the Bible is really saying—which of course leads us right back to the same problem.

If you ask me the whole business of speaking for God has become very confusing. Some people, mainly the religious sort, still hold to the old idea that God speaks through the Bible and through people in one way or another, even though sorting that out can be very messy. Other people seem to have given up on that idea altogether and say that no one speaks for God. These people are left to form their own ideas about God, if they are inclined toward that sort of thing. And as you might expect, most of them create an idea of God that lines up best and easiest with what they hope might be true about the Creator of the Universe.

So now we live in a world where some people are still looking for prophets to tell them the truth about God, and others are determined that no one is going to tell them anything about God ever again.

This is the world in which you and I live. It is the world in which we are all trying our best to figure out if there is a God and what that God might want from us.

And I might be a false prophet in that world.

Which would suck.

I started wondering about this because I got an email from a guy who is absolutely convinced that I am indeed a false prophet.

That's weird, wild stuff, by the way, when someone accuses you of being a false prophet.

Many of you do not believe in prophets, true or otherwise, so I expect you would simply laugh this off and go about your business. But if you are a Christian and another Christian feels that you are a false prophet, you are honor-bound to hear him out and consider the possibility. At least you should do so if the person making the accusation is reasonable.

I'll say this for the guy. He was nice about it. Well, as nice as one can be when delivering that kind of news. I could tell he wasn't enjoying telling me I was a false prophet, and I appreciated that. Having been accused of being a false prophet a few times now, I can tell you that it's a lot easier to take when you can at least know that the person telling you isn't enjoying himself.

He said, "I cannot tell for certain whether you play the role of false prophet intentionally or not, but nonetheless, play the role you do."

This wasn't some dumb guy either. He was intelligent and sincere. He was very sad that I was a false prophet and worried about it. I could tell he was grieved, and that made me sad too, and a little scared. I think I would enjoy a conversation with this guy, but I don't know if he would be interested. Sometimes when Christians identify a bona fide false prophet they can be a little reluctant to socialize with him.

And who can blame them, really?

So anyway, after I had this whole email conversation with this guy, I got to thinking. How do I know I'm NOT a false prophet? And the truth is, I don't know.

Here are three things I do know.

One:

I know I am a minister, and I write here as a minister, albeit as an offbeat and rather unusual minister who cusses and calls himself Real Live Preacher. I often write about what we might call "spiritual things," so I suppose it would be fair to say that I have taken something of a prophetic role for myself. And some people are certainly taking my words seriously.

That scares the hell out of me, by the way.

Two:

I know that I am being honest when I write about my search for spiritual truth. I do not intend harm. I really only intend to describe my own journey and do not necessarily wish to prescribe it for anyone else.

But of course that is exactly the sort of thing you might expect a false prophet to say, if he were any good at the business of being a false prophet. I expect all the really good false prophets would innocently proclaim that they have only the best of intentions. Moreover, I would expect them to be gentle and kind and very pleasant—all the better to lead you astray.

So I suppose, just to be safe, you ought to disregard point number two. If I were a false prophet, I'd probably be an excellent liar. Let's just move on to number three.

Three:

I make the standard Christian claims about Jesus and how he died for our sins, and I read the bible and try to find the best and most responsible ways of applying its truths to my life. But some of my conclusions, drawn from the New Testament and my own experience, sound a little unusual, at least to people who have only been exposed to narrow slices of Christianity.

For example, I say that doubting God's existence is okay and perfectly acceptable within Christianity as long as the person doubting remains obedient and committed to the Christian path.

I also say that some parts of the Bible have no connection to objective history. In short, I own up to the fact that some of the Bible is myth. This doesn't bother me in the least since I understand myth to be a wonderful way for the Creator to communicate with a great number of people across a wide spectrum of cultures and over a vast amount of time. Archetype, baby! Remember that word. There are mysterious reasons why these stories mean so much to us.

And last, I say that some things in the Bible reflect life in an ancient culture and have no business being crudely applied to our modern lives. I search the Bible for universal truths and willingly accept the burden and responsibility to read it with scholarship and make those calls for myself.

The truth is, there is no other way to read the Bible. You either admit that you read the Bible critically and selectively, or you are lying to yourself and others.

As I understand it, it was these things and, of course, my potty mouth that caused this man to decide that I was a false prophet. And that brings me back to the statement I made in the very beginning. Perhaps I am a false prophet. I really don't know.

So okay.

I began with a difficult question, and here I am at the end with no clear answer and only more questions.

What if there was a false prophet in this world, but he thought he was doing and saying the right things all along? And what if he never really wanted to be a prophet at all, only somehow it happened that people were listening to what he said? What if he came to believe that someone needed to be saying something, so he was willing to give it a shot even though it scared him silly? And finally, what if he really loved God but was wrong about some things, and some people came to believe some wrong things because of him?

Do you think God would love and forgive that false prophet? Do you think God's Grace would cover the sins of his theology?

I hope so. I really, really hope so.

wynken, blynken and nod

Wynken, Blynken, and Nod one night
Sailed off in a wooden shoe—
Sailed on a river of crystal light,
Into a sea of dew.
"Where are you going, and what do you wish?"
The old moon asked the three.
"We have come to fish for the herring fish
That live in this beautiful sea..."

There was a time, long ago, when I had my own little bed beneath a window that overlooked a desert in the westward mountain town of El Paso. In the evening, when the shadows grew long and the heat gave way to the chill of the desert night, the coyotes would sing their lonely songs, and I would wait for sleep.

And on those nights I would gaze with love and painful longing upon a picture book with the very odd title of "Wynken, Blynken, and Nod."

I could not read, so I feasted on the enticing illustrations while the memory of my mother's soft voice caused the words to be born again in my heart. There were three little cherubic, tow-headed boys wearing pastel one-piece pajamas. One of the boys had lost a button, which caused half of his flap to sag and revealed a glimpse of his bottom. Their names were Wynken, Blynken, and Nod. They had paper hats and fishing poles, and they set sail in a tiny wooden shoe, hoping to find all the wonderful and dreamy things that beckon to us from just beyond.

Their little boat rocked and nodded in a twilight sea of stars and clouds and twinkling nets. It was the most beautiful thing I had ever seen, and I began to long for something that I could not name or understand.

As I look back on it, it seems that my heart was made for Wynken, Blynken, and Nod. My soul said "yes" to them and to their journey. I wanted to be on that little boat, sailing those mysterious waters in search of something wonderful and sweet that lives over the horizon and out of our reach. I felt in my heart that

Turtles All The Way Down

there must be a reality beyond us where little boys may sail away in wooden boats and be safely returned if they fall asleep on the way.

Gazing at my book as the darkness fell outside my window, I would sate myself on those images and finally drift off to sleep, my soul full of longing and my heart adrift in a sea of joy with no shoreline and no name. It was like floating in an ocean of little boy worship.

Some years passed, and I grew too old for picture books and childish things. In time I forgot about the little boys in their wooden shoe boat. I never understood what I was looking for, but the mark of that sweet desire would always live in my heart.

I grew to be a man and had children of my own. When my first daughter was three, I lay down in bed with her one night to help her go to sleep. One side of her twin bed was against the wall, and I lay on the other side facing out, making a little space for her in between that was almost like a little boat, if you think about it. She fidgeted and kicked and talked to me for a few minutes, and then something magical happened.

She forgot I was there and lost herself in pure play while I faded away like the bedroom furniture in "Where the Wild Things Are." She talked and played with "Sungy," her favorite stuffed bear. I listened, delighted and amazed. She rolled back and forth, bumping into me and sometimes leaning against my body while my eyes closed with delight. I have always loved the feeling of my children's bodies pressed against mine. I love to feel their squirming. A leg flopped over my hip for a moment, and a little hand played in my hair which had become a forest at the top of a mountain. Tiny fingers picked at my shirt and sneaked into one of my pockets looking for candy.

I was treated to the subconscious, slumgullion speech that is common to children who are lost in the absolute present moment of play.

"Do you want to buy an O, round and sweet? No, I don't, because you shouldn't say that. The dolphins are jumping and Sungy says that his mommy doesn't let him say that or buy Os because they're very scary."

Cartoon sound bites and bits of commercials. Little moments from her day. Fears and joys remembered. Scat singing. Noises that amuse. This is your little girl. Listen, for this is how her mind works. Keep silent and know her deepest desires. Strolling through the interior castle of her mind was a most delightful and relaxing pleasure.

Sailing away at bedtime became something I looked forward to. It always happened in the same way. I would listen to her talk and feel her body moving in the bed behind me. In time her voice would grow soft and her breathing would become regular. The squirming would slow and then cease. If I was lucky, the little heel thrown over my hip would grow heavy and not be taken away. She would drift off to sleep, and sometimes I would too, knowing real peace and contentment, if only for that hour.

I have sailed the sleepy-time seas with three daughters now, my own little Wynken, Blynken, and Nod. There were times when more than one of them wanted me to come and see them off to sleep. In those days I thought this journey would last forever. But now my youngest is seven, and she doesn't play with toys in bed anymore. Last night I lay beside her as she read a "Junie B. Jones" book. I asked her to read aloud so that I could hear her voice, but she said, "Dad, I mostly just read silently now."

Oh.

I see.

The last of the three sisters has come of age and put away these childish things. No more sailing away at night on a sea of silly words and playtime. She would rather get a kiss and a hug and be left alone to enjoy her book.

I understand.

It's okay. It really is. One day I may sail the seas of dreamland with a grandchild. One never knows. In the meantime, I take comfort in knowing that I have finally named the thing I longed for so long ago in my bed beneath the window.

It was the journey. It was the journey itself that stirred my heart. It was the boat and the boys and the stars and the sea. It was everything found and felt along the way.

It was always the journey.

It will always be the journey.

I know nothing but the journey.

Whatever calls to us from beyond the horizon of our hearts is hidden for now. There are hints about its nature and stories about its ways in the old books, but what lies beyond the sea remains a mystery. It is the journey that we long for and only the journey that we may know.

Why we love to sail toward something that can never be found is one of life's great mysteries. It's the way we are made, I believe, and I take comfort in that.

> *Wynken and Blynken are two little eyes,*
> *And Nod is a little head,*
> *And the wooden shoe that sailed the skies*
> *Is a wee one's trundle-bed.*
> *So shut your eyes while mother sings*
> *Of wonderful sights that be,*
> *And you shall see the beautiful things*
> *As you rock in the misty sea,*
> *Where the old shoe rocked the fishermen three:*
> *Wynken,*
> *Blynken,*
> *And Nod.*

there's something about the way you use the bible

There's something about the way you use the Bible, something about the way you use it as a tool, as a weapon, as a fulcrum, as a means, as an end, as a trump card.

There's something about your intensity and your urgency and the way you have your eyes locked on some distant prize. There's something about the energy you are putting into this. It's making you frantic and in a hurry. You will not be present in a sacred moment. You will not wait. You will not keep silence. You will not admit that you are weak. You will not let things unfold.

You cannot abide, so you will not abide. You will not abide the journey. Arriving is all you want, and the Bible is some kind of shortcut for you. You seem to be cutting corners and covering your tracks with memorized verses. You enter every room with a blast of pretty Jesus words and a lot of fast talking.

Somehow you have come to think that the Bible is like everything else in your life. You think it is something to master and something you can own. The more you know about the Bible, the more power you hope to gain. The more verses you can quote, the closer to God you hope to be.

The Bible is your prop and your flag. You wave it around and make sure that it is seen. You highlight it and talk about it and make wild claims about its truth and fight over it and win with it and boast about how you believe every word of it. It is your way and your truth and your life.

Behold your sacred battle cry: "The Word of the Lord is living and active, sharper than any two-edged sword, piercing until it divides soul from spirit, joints from marrow; it is able to judge the thoughts and intentions of the heart."

But that verse isn't about the Bible. It's about Christ, whom you serve, and whose spirit you are called to carry in your heart. It is only He who is your way and your truth and your life.

That old man that you brushed aside? The one you called a liberal and a wishy-washy Christian? He spent the last fifty years with his hands and his heart in the pages of that sacred book. He has wept over it and searched for truth in its stories. His unanswered questions have increased every year until finally he knows nothing at all but the love of God and neighbor.

He knows something that you do not know.

Those people around the table? The ones you spoke so harshly to that night when you came upon them sharing a meal and pleasant conversation at church? You told them it was a shame when Christians gathered only to eat and talk. You dropped your big black Bible on the table with a thud for emphasis. They are some of God's oldest and wisest servants. They have prayed down the walls of prejudice and broken the strongholds of anger and pain with the prayers of their hands and feet. Their meal was a prayer, though you couldn't hear it.

They know something that you do not know.

These people know that the Bible is not a self-help book full of easy answers, but a book of stories and wisdom that is meant to lead us into relationship and worship. There are hard and fast truths in it, yes, but they are surrounded by soft truths, and slippery truths, and sometimes truths, and truths that once were true but are no longer true, and truths that are only true if you are in the right state of mind, and truths that are only true if you are not hurting someone, and truths that are true in the moment but not if you are talking about the moment, and truths that can only be lived and should never be spoken, and truths that we cannot hear, and truths that are more than we can bear.

The truths of the Bible are utterly beyond anyone who seeks to own truth and who seeks truth above the Spirit of God.

The Bible is not a book for those who need a weapon. It is not a book for those who know where they are going and what questions they will ask. It is not a book for those who are in a hurry and looking for the shortest route.

The Bible is a book for pilgrims and wanderers. It is a book for children and for those who wish to become children again. It is a book for seekers and searchers and dreamers.

It is a book for anyone and everyone who hopes that the desires of God might be written upon their hearts.

tidings from a pine seed angel

My parents' home in Marshall, Texas is surrounded by ninety-six trees on a one-acre lot, many of them pines towering seventy-five feet or more above the ground, covering the house with a peaceful, green canopy. These giant pines are beautiful but deadly. Now and then an unbalanced growth pattern or a particularly savage storm disrupts the delicate balance of one of these trees, causing it to topple. The tree leans and the ground bulges. Roots snap with gunshot concussions as the tree begins to fall. It picks up speed as it plummets, stripping branches from its neighbors and crushing everything in its path as it settles violently into its final resting place.

The house has yet to sustain a direct hit, but one seems inevitable given the number of trees. Mother Nature is obviously determined to take back her land. Thankfully, she seems to be in no hurry and is apparently not a very good shot.

On occasion I lay myself down upon my father's manicured grass and gaze with wonder at the tops of these pine trees, as they bend and sway in the breeze. There is a deep and powerful groaning when giant trees bend. It is an earth mantra that will drive all but the most jaded of souls into a state of prayer. Lying on your back in a grove of trees is a rare and awe-inspiring pleasure. *If anyone asks you repeatedly why you do this, let that person be to you as a gentile and a tax collector. There's no talking to some people.*

I was in this very posture of restful worship when my eye caught a fluttering movement near the top of one of the pines. A weathered cone cracked open in the heat and finally gave up its precious bounty, allowing a single seed to fall. A tiny, winglike membrane attached to the seed caused it to whirl in the air like a helicopter, spinning it round and round as it descended from on high like an angel coming down a spiral staircase.

I watched the flight of this seed, charmed and fascinated, until I saw it come to rest in my father's lawn. The aging tree's ejection of a single tiny seed struck me as a desperately hopeful gesture. The tight blades of grass prevent these seeds from reaching the soil, and in any case the weekly visits from my father's lawnmower will not allow baby pines to grow.

The environment at the bottom of this grove is no longer suited for procreation. Gone is the tangled undergrowth that once provided shade. Gone is the bedding of needles that once protected seedlings from the cold. Gone are the trunks of ancient ancestors, decaying slowly into rich and scented mulch. And gone are the saplings that once dotted the ground at the base of these trees in a wonderfully haphazard pattern.

The nursery of the old woods was graded long ago and turned into something pleasing to human eyes. My father's yard is beautiful, but there is a disturbing sterility in the landscaping, with its overbearing symmetry, its brick borders, and the "chit, chit, chit" of the sprinklers.

In spite of the hopeless situation below, the trees remain ever faithful to their calling and fill the air with their spinning, angel seeds. Some fall on the driveway and are swept away. Others fall on the asphalt road and die in the shimmering heat. Still others fall on the grass and are shredded and sucked into the lawnmower bag. There seems to be no fertile soil for the seedlings of these ancient and dignified sowers, though their own presence bears witness to a long-forgotten day when the yield was a hundredfold.

Still they launch their floating angels, each one bearing a gospel tiding of hope. The fidelity of these trees to the calling of the Grand Creator stirs my heart and then breaks it.

If things continue in this way, with trees falling every year and none taking root, the day will come when there will be no native-born trees around this house. It will look like the houses in the new subdivisions, with thick grass and store-bought saplings that seem more like pets than trees, utterly dependent on humans for water and fertilizer and held erect with staked cords.

I think the situation seems hopeless for these East Texas Pines, but then I see the world with human eyes and a human sense of time. The ancient trees drop their seeds with a detached dignity, apparently unaware and unconcerned about what we humans are doing down below. Trees take the long view. Someday humans will be gone from this place and the house demolished or crushed under the weight of massive trunks. A winged seed may catch an errant breeze and drift in from a nearby lot to settle into the tattered remnants of my parents' lawn. Sheltered by fallen leaves and wind-blown debris, one of these seedlings may finally take root, signaling the beginning of something new.

And what of me, the man in the grass at the bottom of the grove, who watched these events with momentary interest before going back inside for a second helping of lunch? What of this man?

I would be faithful like the trees, with a gospel as impossible and hopeful, and a method as childlike and innocent. I would take the long view that is beyond me and outside of my simple vision. I would draw upon the promise of power and renewal that comes with faith and faithfulness and leads me to grace and gracefulness.

And I would know my place and my purpose in this world.

And knowing would be enough.

Foy Davis is a fictional character that I created in 2005 when I began writing short stores about his life. I have not written these stories in chronological order, so his life has unfolded slowly over the years and in a rather haphazard manner. There are stories from his childhood, his adolescence, his days as a priest, and after he left the ministry.

I have no organized plan for the Foy stories. I'm not inclined to weave them into a novel. For some reason, I feel resistant to making that kind of a tight narrative about his life. Perhaps I'll just continue to write stories about him, slowly filling in some of the gaps in his life while leaving others open. If that's what I do, I suppose we'll come to know Foy the way we come to know real people. Slowly, over time, we'll connect the dots and learn more about him.

All the Foy Davis stories are currently available at _FoyDavis.com_.

childhood like a dream

Foy Davis was born in 1960, in the small West Texas town of Fort Davis, which lies within a triangle formed by the cities of Van Horn, Fort Stockton, and Marfa. When he was young, his father told him the town was named for Colonel Davis, a distant ancestor of theirs who fought the Indians with great passion and vigor, right up until the moment he ran off to join them and was never heard from again. A few arrowheads and a leather bag were produced as evidence of the story, but none of it was true. The Davis family was new to the area, his father having arrived in 1956 with his new bride.

Foy's father came to be the associate pastor of the Baptist church at the end of Bloys Avenue, which was unpaved then and remains so today. The family's house was fifty yards east of the church, around a little curve in the road. It was a yellow plaster house with a metal roof and a small corner porch with concrete steps. The house was modest enough, but the view from the backyard (if you could call dirt and sand a backyard) was spectacular. The foot of the Davis mountains—also named for Colonel Davis, according to his father—lay no more than one hundred yards from the house. These were desert mountains, brutal mountains. Rocks and outcroppings jutted toward the sky at harsh angles. The sand and the scrubby, barbed plants blistered in the summer heat without trees to shade them. Foy's father used to say this was real desert, none of your sissy deserts like they have down below San Antonio and Uvalde.

Coyotes ate Foy's first dog, so said his father, and it may well have been true. She went into heat and disappeared one night when the coyotes' howls were particularly close. A second dog was purchased and met with the same fate. Coyote cries at night, no dog in the morning. After that Foy and his younger brother were given a guinea pig. It was left out in the sun one afternoon and suffered some sort of heat-stroke. It never took another step, but stood, blinking, wherever it was, until someone picked it up and carried it to another spot. The Davis family did not have good luck with animals.

When Foy was three he used to lay in bed at night and listen to the sounds of the desert that trickled in through the open window. He stared into the darkness until he made himself see green and red lights. He flew the lights around the room in formation, until one night they got out of control and he couldn't shut them off. At least that's how he remembered it. He would pick his nose at night and reach over in the darkness to wipe the mess on the wall. Once it left his hand it was gone completely, as if it never existed. No other possibility occurred to him, until his father bellowed from the room one morning. It was his first philosophy lesson. Things still exist after you let go of them in the darkness. Their existence is not dependent on you. It was the first of many Copernican revolutions, and the new idea was so pleasurable that it overcame even his fear of his father. He watched, mouth agape in wonder, as his father scrubbed the wall.

When he was five, Foy's nose began to bleed regularly because of the dry climate. His father was a kind man and overall a good parent, but he had a tendency to insist on using his personal treatments for ailments and physical problems. Ignoring their protests, he pulled his boys' teeth with a string because he was convinced it was the best way. Get it over and be done with it. He told Foy the best thing for his nosebleeds was to get the inside of his nose cauterized. No reason to fool around with bloody noses when the doctor can fix it right up. Having lost battles like this in the past, Foy made a private vow never to be seen with a bloody nose. He would squat behind the shed and let the blood drip into the dirt until it stopped of its own accord. Then he covered it with sand, like a cat. His parents never found out about that, nor did they know that Foy ate seven or eight tablespoons of white sugar every morning for breakfast. When his mother wasn't looking, Foy would scoop spoonfuls of sugar onto his Rice Crispies and shake the bowl until the sugar settled to the bottom. He would skim his spoon along the surface and eat cereal until his mother turned away. Then he used his spoon to dredge the bottom of the bowl for the good stuff.

Periodically Foy's grandparents would appear for a visit. Their journey from deep East Texas, where both of Foy's parents grew up, was epic—almost a thousand miles after a swing far south into the Rio Grande Valley to buy grapefruit. His grandfather never lost his excitement about grapefruit. It absolutely thrilled him and was certainly worth the extra 250 miles. He said the Ruby Red from the Valley was the greatest grapefruit in the world and grown right there in Texas. Foy loved the grapefruit, but he was bothered by the strange membrane that separated the sections, visible after he spooned out the meat. It didn't seem right that something like that should be in any way connected to food.

His grandparents always brought Foy and his brother a new pair of boots, which was an occasion for great celebration, so much so that in time Foy developed the vague impression that they only made boots back East, an idea that stuck with him much longer than you might imagine. Once his grandfather brought dry ice and put it in water so that a ghostly fog bubbled out of the glass. It was the most wonderful thing Foy had ever seen. All of these things—the grapefruit, the boots, and the dry ice—gave him the idea that far away, in distant lands, were exotic mysteries and wonderful things to behold. This impression stayed with Foy for as long as he lived, and as an old man he would weep when he saw pictures of places he knew he would never visit.

His grandparents liked the climate in Fort Davis. It was hot, but the lack of humidity made it cool in the evenings. His grandfather never tired of pointing out that theirs was a dry heat and not nearly as difficult to manage as the heavy, humid heat of East Texas. Now that was real heat. This aggravated Foy's father, who was a straight thermometer man and believed you should look at the number on the thermometer and not factor in modern notions like humidity. The men in the family had a powerful need to claim the bragging rights that came with living in the most rugged and difficult part of Texas. Though Foy would grow up to be very self-aware and laugh at this trait, even he could not escape it. All of his life he enjoyed telling people about his dogs.

"We lived out in the wild parts of Texas. Out West. The coyotes ate my first dog. Got another dog and they ate him too."

He enjoyed the horrified stares that this comment often brought and the way it tended to silence the conversation. He was bested only once, by an old man in his church in San Antonio who claimed he was strapped to a dental chair in Van Horn when he was twelve and had his tonsils removed without anesthesia. Tonsil care was a part of dentistry in those days, apparently.

"They made me drink Co-Cola when they was done, to cauterize it. It burned like the devil going down."

That time it was Foy who was silenced and stared, horrified. Of course, cauterizing always did give him the heebie jeebies.

When Foy's mother was very old, long after his father had died, Foy asked her if she believed in God. He had always wondered about that but for some reason had never gotten around to asking. It was part of a secret they shared that the question didn't need to be asked. She was so old when he finally brought it up that it was obvious the question came from pure curiosity and nothing else. He knew she would understand that.

Foy and his mother shared a way of looking at the world, a way of thinking and being. When he was young she nurtured his mind behind the scenes. She played the church hostess, pouring coffee for her husband and the deacons while they discussed theology and church things. She sat smiling, letting the men talk while she fed Foy philosophical tidbits under the table. The Sunday School teachers swaddled his mind every Sunday morning with church wisdom and church ideas. On Sunday nights she took him outside under the stars. There, under the glitter of the world's most ancient wisdom, she carefully unwound the swaddling clothes and set him free.

She wasn't a hypocrite or a liar. She went to church every Sunday with the family. She wanted to go. But she did not want her son bound and trapped as she had been. She wanted his mind to be free. She read science books to him. She taught him the constellations. She bought him a microscope. She probed his mind with trick questions, teaching him to think.

"Foy, are squares real?"

"Of course."

"How do you know? Have you ever seen one?"

"Yes, they're everywhere. All over the place."

"That's funny, because I've never seen a square. And I've been looking for them all of my life."

She explained to him that there was no such thing in all the world as a perfect square, and of course only perfect squares count as squares. When the truth of this became clear to him, he was as filled with joy as she was.

"Then why do they teach us about squares in school if there really aren't any?"

"That," she said with a satisfied smile, "is a good question."

Once she asked him what he thought the number four was. He knew her game by then, so he said, "What do YOU think it is?"

"I don't know, but something feels wrong about it. I know what it means that there are four marbles or four chairs, but I'm realizing that I don't know what FOUR is. Is four something in and of itself?"

The two of them sat together, trying to wrap their minds around the question.

It seemed like something was indeed missing from the idea of four. What was four?

She said, "Maybe it's just the state of being that happens whenever there are four of anything in a defined area. Four is what IS whenever four things are."

Then she giggled. "What a strange world," she said.

Foy's mother was the first in her family to go to college. Her grandfather was a sharecropper. Three of her father's seven siblings died, one while the family was on the way to California after their farm failed. Her father came back to Texas, married, and went to work selling shoes in Conroe. He was smart but uneducated. She was his only daughter, and his dream was that she would go to college, which she did. She went to college to become a teacher, because that's what girls did in their world. Then she took a philosophy course and was hooked. She changed her major to philosophy but kept it a secret from everyone. She took up smoking and lived for two years in the world of the mind, where the only things that mattered were romantic, metaphysical ideas. Her senior year she was offered a fellowship to pursue a master's degree in philosophy, but she turned it down. She had fallen in love with a young man who was heading for seminary. It was the mid-fifties, and she lived in Texas. It seemed like a noble thing to stop dreaming and get on with real life, which was having children and being properly religious. Any regret or resentment she felt about this was strictly latent. Unconscious. Deep stuff. At every conscious level, she celebrated her life.

She did, however, keep her philosophy textbooks. And she was ferociously protective of them. Foy's father once suggested that she get rid of them. Her response displayed an anger wildly out of proportion to his suggestion. He said she could keep her crazy books if that made her happy, and he never mentioned them again. She kept them neatly arranged on the shelves in his study with his theology books. The Greeks first, the cosmological thinkers of the 17th and 18th centuries, the 19th century Germans, existentialism, British empiricism…and then the collection stopped. That's as far as she had gotten in college. Over the years her books grew outdated and brittle. Most were out of print. Having been pressed together for years, the covers fit each other perfectly, like fingers on a hand. Occasionally she would flip through them to bone up in case philosophy ever came up in a conversation. It never did. The people they knew in Fort Davis were not interested in such things.

Not long after Foy was born, his mother went out into the backyard with a red light and an astronomy book. She came in hours later, thoughtful. Foy's father asked if anything was wrong. She looked at him for a few moments, then decided this was not a conversation that would come to anything. "No," she said. "Everything is fine."

Later that week she removed her books from his shelves and put them in the living room, near the porch. It had an odd name, the living room, since no one did much living there. The children were not allowed on the furniture. She imagined that this was the place where intelligent guests would gather to play the piano and talk over coffee. She kept this room immaculately clean and often rearranged her ancient books, like a boy sorting through his baseball cards. Her philosophy collection remained there until after she died, when Foy took the books to his home. He smelled them with great affection and put them on his own bookshelves, between Systematic Theology and Jung, where they seemed to find a place of individuated harmony after all the years of schism.

Foy's mother was 80 years old when he asked her if she believed in God. He was 55.

"Do I believe in God?" She stared into space for a few moments with her mouth open.

"You know, I've never been able to answer that question because I've never been able to figure out what the question means. I don't really know what it means to believe in God. Is that just thinking the right things about God or do emotions factor into it as well? What if a person loved God SO much—just the whole idea of God—but if you pressed her, what if she admitted that she wasn't sure that God was real? Would that person be a believer or an unbeliever? What if you believed in God, say, three times a week on average, for several years. Just three or four times a week you'd say, 'Yes, there has to be a God.' But then other times it didn't seem like there was a God. You see what I mean? I know this sounds silly, but I still don't understand the question. Everybody else seems to have answered the God question by the time they were ten or twelve, and run to the ends of the earth with their answers. And here I am still trying to figure out the question. And now, Foy, I'm old. I'll die an old sinner, a silly old woman who always over-thought everything, until it was a wonder I made any decisions at all."

Tears appeared in her eyes. Foy put his arm around her.

"It's okay mom. It doesn't matter. I like that about you, that you don't always have stuff figured out. I'm sure that God is very…pleased with…that kind of honesty. And as far as I'm concerned…"

She pulled away from him and seized his arm.

"I will tell you this. I never gave my soul to anyone. They didn't get it. Not your father or the church or science or any other man-made thing. I saved it for God, if there is a God. My soul is as innocent and tender as a peach. And it's ripe for the picking. God can pick it himself, if he wants it, thank you very much. I don't need any damn middle men."

It was the first and only time he ever heard her curse. They stared at each other for a few moments, then burst into laughter at the same time. They laughed so hard that Foy started to choke. Then it all turned to tears and he wept. His mother pulled him close and laid his head against her chest.

"My boy," she said between laughs.

savage joy

About a decade ago I glanced into my middle daughter's room and found her sitting on her knees, looking out the window with her favorite toys lined up on the windowsill. They were all there: her blanket—which had a personality and a loose seam for a mouth—various plush animals, a number of Disney characters, a group of small horses, and an assortment of other figures. She had turned her little friends toward the glass as if they were all looking out into the front yard together. She was talking with them, perhaps drawing their attention to something in the yard, or maybe holding court on any number of intimate subjects.

I immediately froze and did not make a sound. This was my second child, so I was an experienced enough parent to know a precious and unrepeatable thing when I saw it. I leaned against the door frame, then let my body slide slowly down the frame until I was on my knees.

She talked to her toys, jabbering about one thing and then another. She moralized, corrected, parented, acted out parts. She was lost in the Kingdom of Shelby, a place made up of bits and pieces of her life tossed about in her mind and dreams. Her kingdom was not governed by rules or laws or physics. The glue holding Shelby's kingdom together was her own frail and developing view of the world. It was an infantile worldview without borders or categories, at least none that you or I would recognize.

I say "was" because Shelby is now a teen-ager, so she has been banished from the Kingdom of Shelby except at night when all the old things return from the deep waters and shadowed forests of dreaming.

All children have their own play world, and they are able to lose themselves in it. The state of play exists before consciousness. It is an indescribable and intensely personal thing for a child to be deep in play. And if they find they are being watched, they will come back from that world and become shy or start performing. Either way, the magic is lost.

I was peeking into the Kingdom of Shelby, and you can bet I wasn't going to miss the show. I listened, leaning against the doorframe, absolutely enraptured by the sounds of her play. I suppose I was as lost in the moment as she was.

I would have stayed for hours. You couldn't have dragged me away. Eventually a prolonged silence caused me to open my eyes. She was looking at me with a smile.

"Hi Daddy."

She was friendly, but clearly waiting for me to leave so that she could go back to her world. I had intruded, and it was time for me to go. Shelby was a kindly landowner, who would let you pick an apple and give you a cold drink if you wandered onto her property, but she would definitely show you the way to the gate.

I knew that about her. And I knew there was no use trying to prolong the moment or—God forbid—trying to recreate it.

I was drawn to my little girls in those days in ways that are quickly fading as the three sisters grow into young women. Our biological connection showed itself in my love of the smell of their scalps, my physical and intense need to hold them, and my desire to feel their small bodies pressed against my own as we watched movies together on the couch. And I always had a strong attraction to the sounds they made. Their voices were a kind of OM for me, a sound from below all sounds, a noise from the foundation of my existence. Hearing my daughters play was a joyful thing, and the ache of its absence will never heal. It is a wound I will carry as long as I walk this earth.

The best things are like this, aren't they? They are savage and untamed. Like a great sunset, they can be discovered by chance and enjoyed, but never owned. Like love they can be received but not bought. The best things in life ride a ticklish wave along the surface of your skin, leaving raised hairs in their wake. They move through the world leaving no visible sign. You cannot follow them, nor anticipate their direction and wait for them in a blind.

You will come across spontaneous, unique moments of joy like this now and again. They are Life's gifts to us all. They come to the washed and the unwashed, to the common and the sophisticated, to the rich and the poor, to the just and the unjust.

Moments of savage joy are there for all of us to find. If you haven't seen one lately, you only need to slow down a bit and keep your eyes open. I can give you no counsel beyond that. But if you come across a moment of wild, untamed joy, for God's sake eat it; drink it; hear it; receive it. This is the stuff of life. It doesn't get any better.

where is the man?

A Real Live Preacher Dramatized Version.

The two men in expensive robes looked very out of place in the darkest part of the back streets, but they were not afraid. Their robes and their attitude let everyone know who they were. No one would dare harm them, even at night.

"Do we understand one another?"

"Yes, separate one. I understand perfectly."

One of the robed men tossed a few coins into the shadows of a doorway. As they turned to walk away he called back over his shoulder.

"Don't be late. And don't disappoint me!"

They walked quickly through the alleys with the sleeves of their robes pressed over their noses and mouths. The man who had thrown the coins said to his companion, "A most distasteful business, I must say."

🙟 🙟 🙟 🙟 🙟

Jesus came early to the temple the next morning to continue his discussions with a small crowd of people made up mostly of tradesmen from the streets of Jerusalem. They were thrilled that this exciting young rabbi seemed to enjoy teaching regular people. Soon they were knotted around Jesus and engaged in a passionate discussion of the Torah and its interpretation.

Their conversation was interrupted by the panicked shrieks of a woman. All heads turned at the same time to see a group of about ten men pushing their way through the crowd and up to the front where Jesus stood. These were important and very religious men, some of them scholars and officials of the Temple. Others were Pharisees, respected and wealthy men who took pride in keeping themselves away from sinners.

The townspeople around Jesus parted respectfully, allowing the men to the front. Two were dragging a woman along with them. They thrust her violently toward Jesus, and the crowd drew back further when they saw her.

The woman stood with her head down and her hair covering most of her face. Her shoulders were hunched inward with shame, and she was desperately holding a tattered robe around her body. Her feet were bare and her hair was dirty. She was disheveled and confused, and she was not properly covered. A glimpse of her thigh was visible through a fold in the cloth. Under her chin the robe sagged, revealing her collar bone.

One of the Pharisees stepped boldly forward and spoke directly to Jesus. "Honored rabbi, this woman was caught in the very act of adultery."

He paused and looked around at the crowd for effect before repeating himself loudly.

"In the VERY ACT! Her guilt is beyond question. We bear witness to it. Now the law of Moses says that we should stone her here and now. But of course, with Jesus here at the temple today, we are fortunate to have an expert opinion on matters of the Law. We wouldn't want to act hastily. After all, a woman's life is at stake."

He cocked his head slightly and stretched his arm out toward Jesus with his palm up.

"So I ask you, rabbi, what do YOU say we should do?"

He said the word "rabbi" with mock intensity, drawing it out until it almost sounded like an insult.

Jesus looked at the group of religious men before him. They met his gaze without looking the slightest bit uncomfortable or unsure of themselves. He turned his head and looked at the small crowd of people who moments before had been listening to him teach and asking questions. They were all looking at him now. Some of them were nodding to each other as if to say, "Yes, I'd like to know what Jesus says about a terrible thing like this."

Then Jesus turned his eyes to the woman who stood trembling before them all. His eyes moved slowly over her, picking up details that told him something of her story.

She was a woman of the streets; that seemed obvious. She looked hard and desperate. The bottoms of her feet were calloused and thickened, as were the fingers clutching the edges of her cheap robe. She had known hard labor, and the life she now lived made her harder still. Her hair was dirty and there was straw in it. It looked as if someone had thrown her to the ground, tossed the robe at her, and given her a few seconds to make herself presentable.

But something was wrong here. Something was missing. Something nagged at the blurry edges of his awareness, something he couldn't quite put his finger on.

Jesus slowly lowered himself into a squatting position, eyes still on the woman. Then he looked at the ground before him and wrote with his finger in the dust as he thought and wondered. The crowd was quiet. They stared at him and wondered what he was going to do next.

And then he froze. His index finger stopped moving in the dirt. He understood. He knew what was missing. His eyes closed and he let the air out of his lungs with a groan. His shoulders sagged. He became intent on the ground before him, and he wrote in the dirt, "Where is the man?"

He stood quickly and stepped across what he had written and toward the Pharisee who seemed to be the ringleader. He spoke directly to him, but loud enough for everyone to hear.

"Where is the man?"

"What man?"

"You know what man. It does take two to commit adultery. Why have you not brought him here to face justice alongside her?"

The Pharisee's face tightened with anger. "The whereabouts of the man are not your concern here today. You call yourself a rabbi, do you not? We have come to you with a legitimate question of the law and of justice. Answer please, honored rabbi. What is to be done with this adulteress who stands before you in obvious guilt? Answer and perhaps we shall talk about the man when we are done with her."

Jesus narrowed his eyes and stepped forward again until he was standing right in the face of the Pharisee. Years of carpentry work had made Jesus strong. He had broad shoulders and rough hands. But the Pharisee was unafraid. There could be no greater triumph for him than if Jesus were to strike him down.

But Jesus made no violent move toward him. Instead, he spoke softly in a voice that only the two of them could hear.

"You set this up, didn't you? Yes, of course you did. How does one catch a woman in the very act of adultery, I wonder? How unless he knows ahead of time when it is going to take place. How much did you pay him? I wonder how a man like you even knows how to find people who will do things like this."

The Pharisee looked calm and spoke in a whisper. "The crowd awaits your answer, rabbi."

Jesus turned and took three steps back to the side of the woman who had not moved or lifted her head. Her hair still screened her face, perhaps giving her some small feeling of privacy. Jesus stood for a few moments looking at the place in the dirt where he had written "Where is the man?"

Then he addressed the crowd in a loud voice.

"You have called me rabbi, and I willingly accept that title and all that goes with it. You have come to hear my judgment in this matter. Very well, my judgment I will give as long as you pledge to honor it."

The ringleader squinted and looked suspicious, but the other religious leaders and many in the crowd were nodding in agreement. What he said seemed fair enough.

Jesus bent down and picked up a fist-sized rock. He bobbed it up and down in his hand, feeling its weight, and then he spoke again.

"This is what I say. She is guilty, so stone her according to the Law of Moses. Yes, stone her now and let God's justice be done!"

The woman screamed in terror, and the crowd exploded into frantic whispers. Everyone was talking at once. The Pharisee who had asked Jesus for judgment smiled. He had never in his wildest dreams expected such an easy and complete victory.

Many in the crowd were shocked and uncomfortable. Although the Law of Moses indeed specified this penalty for her offense, public stoning was rare and frowned on by the Roman government. Many would say that stoning was right, but few had the stomach to cast stones themselves. No one knew how to proceed. Even the religious leaders who brought this woman to Jesus did not think that he would say such a thing. Jesus was supposed to be an advocate of mercy for common people. He was known to associate and even eat with women like this.

Jesus used the confusion of the crowd to maximum effect. He slowly raised the rock over his head and faced the woman. The crowd became silent. All eyes were on him. Then Jesus turned to the man in the fancy robe, the Pharisee.

"You have heard my judgment. Now hear my terms. Let the first man to cast a stone be a man who is himself guilty of no sin! And let him come forward now, before us all, and claim his right to take this rock and carry out this justice."

With that Jesus hurled the rock at the feet of the ringleader. It hit the ground with a loud thud. Then Jesus squatted back down and resumed writing in the dust by the feet of the woman.

The crowd was stunned. Many stood with their mouths hanging open.

Some of the townspeople, empowered by Jesus, nodded in agreement. After a few moments everyone began leave. Some of the religious leaders melted into the crowd and left as well.

Jesus never looked up. He kept his eyes on the ground as the crowd dispersed. In the end, the only one left was the man who had brought the accusation. Feeling his power slipping away, he turned and left himself, uttering a barely audible oath as he walked away.

Jesus squatted in silence beside the woman. When he looked up they were alone. He rose to his feet and spoke to her.

"Daughter of Abraham, lift up your head and look around you."

"I cannot."

"Then lift up your eyes at least and see who condemns you now."

Slowly, the woman's hand pulled her matted hair away from her eyes. She looked around, amazed to find that there was no one left but her and Jesus.

"Who is left to condemn you?"

"No one, sir."

"Then neither do I condemn you. Go your way and be at peace."

She pulled her robe more tightly around her shoulders, dropped her hair into her eyes again, and began to walk away.

"Daughter of Abraham. I have something to say to you before you go."

She stopped, but she did not turn around or look up.

"Your name is worth more than this; do not dishonor it. Your life is worth more than this; do not waste it."

The woman made a slight move with her head that might have been a nod, then started to walk again. Jesus spoke one last time.

"Daughter of Abraham, YOU are worth more than this. Go now and sin no more in this fashion. Be instead the child of God that you were meant to be."

This time her shoulders shuddered and a soft sob was heard. She ran and disappeared around a corner.

Jesus watched her go and whispered softly to himself, "Go, daughter of Abraham. Go and live your life, for we are all worth more than this."

a short history of martin luther

Note: If you don't know anything about church history and the reformer Martin Luther, you should read "A Short History of Martin Luther" by my 16-year-old daughter before you read this essay. Come to think of it, you should read the thing by my daughter even if you have a PhD in church history. Trust me!

By rlp's 16-year-old daughter

Okay, uh, the thing is that a long time ago—I don't know when but a LONG time ago—there was nothing but Catholics. I mean, in the church. Course there were lots of other kinds of people and stuff, but in the church, yeah. Nothing but Catholics.

Which was cool if you're into the whole Catholicism thing, but then, you know, not everyone is or even WAS back then.

Then the church got kinda messed up. Apparently they were corrupt and all, you know? Like REALLY messed up. And there was this one badass monk guy named Martin Luther. Not Martin Luther King, but another guy and longer ago. Way back. So Martin was like totally disillusioned with the church because they were doing stuff that was just like, SO wrong. Like I think you could pay money and get to commit sins and stuff like that.

So Martin just got fed up with all of it, and he nailed like all these reasons why the church was messed up onto a door on a piece of paper. They had some weird name for them….uh, theses or something but it was just a list of all the things he didn't like about the church. He nailed it on some door—I don't know where—Europe, maybe Sweden or something. Who knows?

Oh, my dad's yelling at me that this was in the 1500s. Dude, that WAS a long time ago!

Anyway, the church officials and leader guys got seriously pissed off about it, and they called him in for this big meeting. It was called—this is hilarious—The Diet of Worms.

I had German last year, and "diet" is like a council or a meeting I think, only that wasn't on the vocabulary list Mrs. Jenkins gave us, but I think that's pretty much what it means. And Worms is the name of this town in Germany. But Worms doesn't mean "worms" in German or anything. It was just a normal word to them, so they wouldn't have laughed at it.

So at this meeting they tried to make Martin Luther take back everything he had written about the bad things the church was doing in all these books he had written or whatever.

Oh, dude, this is totally messed up. Back then? They could kill you, the church could, if you didn't believe all what they believed or at least kept your mouth shut and all. That is so totally uncool.

But Martin—and this is kinda why I said he was a badass monk—he asked to think about his answer all night and in the morning he said, "Here I stand, I can do no other." And he said that even though he might be killed for saying it.

But they didn't kill him, or maybe he escaped or something, but he didn't die. They did kick him out of the church and all, which some people thought it meant you were going straight to hell, so it was pretty serious to them. And after that him and a bunch of other people started the whole Protestant thing. And nowadays Protestants are everywhere—practically the whole world is filled with them. Except of course all the other religions and stuff. I don't really know that much about them.

And my dad says we've pretty much patched things up with the Catholic Church now, so that lots of people who are Christians are at least polite to each other. And that's prolly why I'm allowed to go to this Catholic church with my friend Andrea, and it's a cool church, so…

But I guess that's pretty much it.

martin luther, diet coke, and canned soup

Jung felt that daydreams, like night dreams, contain great personal significance for us. Your unconscious speaks to you both at night and during the day. The exact nature of the unconscious and the meaning of these dreams remain a mystery. But that's where the fun comes in.

I have a recurring daydream that comes to me quite often. I do not understand the significance of it, and if you think you do, I would prefer you keep your thoughts to yourself. I don't really want to know.

This daydream comes mostly when I should be working on a sermon or when I'm in an elevator. In the dream I am showing the 16th century reformer, Martin Luther, the modern world. How he arrived in our century is not a part of my daydream. Nor is there any explanation for why he speaks modern English.

Martin Luther is absolutely astounded by Diet Coke, elevators, and canned soup. And he says that our world smells funny.

I wince as I look at his monk's robe, which certainly has not been washed in this or perhaps any other century. "You're a bit ripe yourself, Marty. But what's an odor or two among brothers in Christ, eh?"

"Well put," he says with a polite nod.

He is startled by the fizzy pop when I open an ice cold Diet Coke. He lifts the can to his ancient lips, and his eyes open wide. Then he bends forward at the waist, spraying foamy suds all over the floor.

"What in the unholy name of Zwingli is this? It burns like a brew straight from the devil's arse!"

"Oh, sorry. That's called carbonation. They have this way of putting bubbles in some of the things we drink. I don't know why we like it, but we do. I guess it's a bit of a shock if you're not used to it."

He squints at the can, sounding out the letters. "'Diet of Coke.' I am not familiar with this particular council. Is there to be a disputation? Will I be asked to defend myself? You understand I'm a bit nervous after the incident at Worms."

"Oh yeah, the Diet of Worms. That's that council meeting where you were excommunicated, right?"

His eyes broke away from mine. He looked around the room, then back at me. He nodded hesitantly.

"Don't worry man, Diet Coke is a whole other thing."

He looked relieved. Then I had a great idea.

"Hey man, SAY it!"

"Say what?"

"You knooooow…" I say, dragging it out enticingly.

"Oh very well. I suppose you'll pester me until I do."

Martin Luther clears his throat and lifts an arm, affecting the posture of an old fashioned orator.

"Here I stand. I can do no other!"

"YES!" I shout, pumping my fist like Tiger Woods does when he sinks a long putt. "Larry is not going to freakin' believe this."

"Larry?"

"Oh yeah, he's a friend of mine, a pastor up in Dallas… uh, this city north of here."

"He's not a Calvinist, is he? Or an Anabaptist? If he is, by God, I shall lay my hands on a stout quarterstaff and beat his head until the mule shite that fills it pours out of his ears."

"Whoa Marty, calm down. Take it easy. He's a Baptist, and that's a group that didn't get started until you were pretty much already dead. And Baptists… well, you don't wanna know. Anyway, we don't really do head pounding as such anymore. Things have calmed down a lot since your time."

To get his mind off quarterstaffs and heresy, I take him on his first elevator ride. He is beside himself with glee and pushes all the buttons. Every time the door opens he thinks we are in a different place and laughs like a madman. A woman in a business suit enters on the 8th floor, frowns when she sees that all the buttons have been pushed, then pushes the lobby button. She glances at Martin Luther, who is trying hard to suppress his giggles, and pushes the lobby button two more times. Then she puts a handkerchief to her nose and gets off on the 7th floor.

For lunch I pull out two cans of Campbell's Beef and Vegetable soup. I toss one to him, enjoying his puzzled look.

"It's soup, Martin. Watch."

I put a can opener along the top and squeeze the handle until it locks. Then I twist it and the can rotates until the top pops off. Martin Luther leans over and watches everything. I pour the soup into a couple of bowls and pop them into a microwave. He puts his forefinger against the glass and fiddles with the buttons a bit while the soup is heating. He is startled by the "ding," and then we have hot soup together.

"It's a bit salty," says he, "but extraordinary, considering it came from those strange cylinders. What did you call them again?"

"Cans."

"And you may simply open one of these CANS whenever you're hungry?"

"Yep."

"Remarkable."

After the soup we both get quiet, and things are a little uncomfortable. Martin Luther picks at his robe, while I make two or three attempts at small talk. After the way he laughed on the elevator, I'm a little worried about showing him anything else.

"So…how much longer will you be here?"

"Not much longer. Just a few more minutes and I have to go back."

"Oh," I say, sadly. "Okay, how about this? We each get to ask the other two questions about life in his time. I go first."

Martin Luther nods in agreement.

This is the opportunity of a lifetime, and I don't want to blow it. But suddenly I can't think of anything to say. And time is running out. I open my mouth and say the first thing that comes to mind.

"What was the longest time you ever went without brushing your teeth?"

"Brushing my teeth? What does that mean?"

"Never mind, that pretty much tells me more than I need to know. Okay, how about this: Why were people in your time so uptight about theology? You killed each other, for God's sake. I mean, literally, FOR THE SAKE OF GOD, you tortured and killed each other. Why?"

Martin Luther answers quickly and with a straight face. "That's easy. We really believed."

Turtles All The Way Down

"Whaddya mean? In God? WE believe in God."

He smiles. "No you don't. Not really. You have so many options. There are so many different things that people in your time can believe. Your belief is a wispy, smoky, light-weighted sort of thing. I can see right through it. People in your world really don't know WHAT they believe. For us, God is as real as rocks and wind and rain and summertime. And because we believe, we are passionate. Too passionate at times, I will admit. I see things much clearer now."

"How do you know that much about us? All you've seen are Diet Cokes, elevators, and canned soup. I mean, we have a whole lot more than that."

Martin Luther smiles. "I've seen enough. And now it's my turn. I have only one question for you."

"Shoot," I say.

He looks puzzled.

"Oh, uh, go ahead and ask."

"Our lives are filled with much hardship. Winters are hard; summers too. Only wealthy people may hear music, and most people cannot read. Just securing food and water takes hours out of our days. In my entire lifetime, I only managed to write a set of commentaries and an assortment of other works and treatises. With your many labor saving devices, your elevators and your canned soup, I imagine that people can accomplish so much more with their lives. I imagine your days are filled with prayer and creation and loveliness. It is a marvelous time in which you live, is it not? Are people fully educated and busily engaged with writing and art and music and philosophy and theology?

I can't think of a way to answer him, and Martin Luther is fading away. I have to speak quickly.

"No, most of us produce very little. We tend to consume a lot, though. We spend most of our time consuming and using things. And we work an awful lot so that we can pay for all the things we want to consume. A lot of us consume more than we can pay for, so we buy on credit. And then of course, we have work doubly hard to pay our creditors. That's just the way it is."

Martin Luther looks puzzled, and just before he fades away he says, "I don't understand what you mean."

He's gone before I can reply, but I speak anyway.

"Yeah, we don't really understand it either, Martin."

depression part one: admitting you might have a problem

My doctor drew a little diagram of a brain and of a nerve pathway with a gap in it. He pushed the paper in front of me so that I could see it.

"You see, this gap prevents unnecessary communication between different parts of your brain. You don't want your thinking to become undifferentiated. When you have certain kinds of experiences, neurotransmitters are secreted into this gap, making the connection and allowing communication from one part of your brain to the other. See?"

One part of me was listening to him, but my eyes kept slipping over to the right side of the paper where he had written a list of symptoms. I couldn't stop looking at the list because I have every single one of them.

He continued. "You're a poster child for this disorder. I'll probably be telling people about you when I describe it in the future. The depression, the loss of energy and a lack of desire to do anything, the anxiety attacks, the migraines, the facial tic, the insomnia, the trouble with digestion, the appetite issues, the dark moods and temper flare-ups. It's textbook.

"That coupled with your family history, your mom and your grandfather. It sounds like he struggled with this his entire life. I won't know for sure until we get your tests back, but I'm convinced you have a chemical deficiency, or imbalance if you want to think of it that way, that runs in your family."

"It's true," I said. "I never want to do anything. I have to make myself do everything, even fun things with the girls. Sometimes I can make myself get started and hope the desire will catch up to me. The only thing I want to do is escape from everyone. Writing and movies do that for me. I got along okay until the last year or so. That's when the facial tic and the bad headaches started.

"Do you know I never want to go to church on Sunday morning? I have to make myself go. It's like whipping a dog and driving him out of the house.

Every Sunday for years. I thought there was something missing in my spirit, you know, like I'm not praying enough or something. I always manage to find a way to get up for the people at church, but I can't seem to get myself together for my own family. They see a different Gordon, one that no one else sees."

Suddenly I began to weep, though I didn't feel like I should be crying. Part of me was standing outside myself, watching and analyzing. "What the hell are you crying for, you fraud?"

The doctor listened patiently, then said, "I know."

I pulled myself together and said, "So, what would it be like if I took whatever it is you're thinking of giving me?"

"Well, it's a matter of trying it and seeing what happens, but I think it would be like coming back to life again. I think you probably don't even realize how diminished life has become for you. You've probably struggled with this for some years now. When people are younger they can usually compensate a little better."

"Yeah...I guess. Look, I'm not sure how to say this, but what's going to happen to the way I think about the world around me? Is this going to change that? I think I tend to experience things in a kind of detached way, almost like I'm watching myself. And then later I write about what's happened to me, and that's when all the emotion comes. Do you think this is going to change the way I think and experience things in some fundamental way?"

"No, I don't. I think you'll come to remember that you used to experience things quite passionately and in the present moment. You've just forgotten. You're not thinking clearly right now. You know, our thoughts and our emotions are tied together very closely. I think taking this medication will bring you back to life."

I wanted to believe that this was true, but some part of me couldn't accept it.

"See, the thing is, I can't help but think this is just a problem that I should be able to cope with. You know, like everyone else does. Taking some drug seems like the lazy way out."

"Is that what you tell people in your church who are on medication?"

"No."

"Of course not, because you know that sometimes people have to take medicine. It's not a matter of the will or of strength. Your brain isn't secreting enough neurotransmitters. We're fortunate to live in a time when medication can help. Your grandfather didn't have this option."

He paused, then went on. "If you want to keep trying to feel better on your own, you can. I can tell you what will happen. It's only going to get worse for you. Your children and your wife will be forced to live with a shadow of who you really are. Eventually it will become too much for you, and you'll probably end up in a hospital like your mom. Sure you're strong and determined, probably as strong as anyone I've met, but eventually this thing will eat your lunch. And what will be the use of that? So what if you manage to hold out for another twenty years or so? You'll only be robbing your family of what they need, which is you."

I wasn't convinced, but I was becoming open to the idea. I still felt like I was just some lazy guy looking for an easy way out. But I went to this doctor promising myself and my wife that I would at least try his advice.

Then he gave me a way out. "If you want to keep trying therapy, you can go to that guy in Austin that you like. You can try it for a few more months, but I don't think it's going to help. You can't talk your body into increasing its production of neurotransmitters."

For a moment I considered putting this off for awhile. I thought about it, but in my mind I saw a picture of myself sitting, slumped on the couch: Lillian skips in and asks if I want to play chess. I feel a wave of irritation that makes no sense at all. "No, I don't want to do anything," I say with no feeling or compassion.

"No. I'm going to continue therapy for other reasons, but I want to give this a try. When can I start?"

Down inside I still wonder if I have a problem that requires medication, but I am a trusting person. I am trusting my doctor. My family is worth at least that.

if only for this i need god

Now and then I become aware that some child has suffered an unspeakable horror. Most of the time, I cannot bear this truth. I quickly turn my mind elsewhere, because I'm too busy or too tired to deal with the reality of evil. My shadow self files this knowledge away in a secret drawer while the conscious part of me sings, "La, la, la, la, la; I can't hear you."

But sometimes I allow myself to hold the knowledge of terrible evil in my mind. I can feel the raging, voracious appetite of evil, the consuming black hatred in it. Evil puts its snarling face right before my own, a leather-clad drill sergeant from hell who spews black flecks of spit all over my face. His breath smells like gas bursting from a swollen carcass.

Usually this is as much as I can handle. I can stand before evil for a few moments with my eyes screwed shut and my face turned away. My mind searches frantically for anything else to think about. Anything else. I mumble panicked baby prayers. "Dear Jesus, sweet Jesus, make it go away!"

But evil is like a deep, sore place inside my tongue. I cannot leave evil alone. Something keeps me gnawing at it, discovering over and over again that yes, this sore spot still hurts like hell.

In these moments of extreme masochism, I manage to push past the drill sergeant and move deeper into the domain of evil. I allow myself to imagine that this horrible thing was done to my middle daughter: my Shelby, my Sharmy, my Sobee, my Tubby Lumpkin. She of the tender heart and loving ways. She sits with her brown eyes on the very edge of womanhood, looking and knowing, cautious and so easily frightened.

I can see the fear in Shelby's eyes and her panicked thrashing. Sometimes I can hear her scream for me. "Daddy," she cries, but I am not there for her.

This is an infinite evil. Thinking of it is like trying to comprehend the size of the universe. It is beyond the capacity of my mind. My defense mechanisms begin to kick in, and I am numbed. Benumbed by evil. I can only shake my head and wonder that any mind could comprehend this reality.

I turn and run. I run from evil as fast as I can, but some impish part of me looks back, like Lot's wife, to see the fire raining down from the sky. In this moment, one final thought makes it through my defenses. And here is that final thought: When any child suffers, it is as tragic and horrible as my own child suffering. And many children suffer in our world. Their screams fill the heavens and surround our planet with a haze of sorrow, a beacon to the universe. "Stay away! This world is broken. These people hurt each other. They always have, and they always will."

This is all I can do, and this I have done. I have gazed into the gaping maw of the devil and smelled his rancid breath. I will not go closer, unless of course, some other person exercises his terrible gift of freedom and makes me enter therein. But for now, yes, this is all I can do.

If only for this I need God. If only to think that somewhere there is a mind that can comprehend evil and does comprehend it; that can count evil and does count it; that can know evil and does know it for what it is. I want evil to be known, and goodness too. I want someone to bear the awful knowledge of good and evil.

But more than that, I want to believe that no child's scream goes unheard.

this is how it happened

You want to know how it happened? I'll tell you how it happened. I got tired. I couldn't do it anymore. I fought an inward battle with orthodoxy for years and tried to figure out what the Bible has to say about this. I took six years of Greek, hoping the original language of the New Testament might shed some light. I got a Bachelor's degree in religious studies and a Master of Divinity. I read everything I could find and talked to everyone I respected. But in the end, it all came down to this – I could not be orthodox in this matter. I could not. So I gave up and gave in. And the minute I did I felt a flood of cool relief, like water after forty days in the desert.

The moment of choice came, and I chose to stand with my friends. That's the deal. That's the way it happened. I wish I could tell you that my rigorous study finally unlocked the secrets of the New Testament's scant witness on this matter, but it never did. For twenty years I asked this question of the Bible and never got a clear answer. Finally, I realized that I could wait on the Bible no longer.

I had to choose my place in the middle of uncertainty, ambiguity, and doubt. I had to make a choice. I had to stand on one side or the other. The bottom line is, I don't give a damn what you think the Bible says. I'm not going to stand against my friends on this. I can't. I cannot. I am unable to stand against them and not collapse from sorrow and despair.

Whatever this says about me, I willingly accept. You say this makes me a liberal? What does a label like that mean when laid alongside real living? You say I don't respect the scriptures? It's been years since I had the energy or the desire to argue about that with anyone. The truth is, I'm okay with any label you want to give me. Only I'm not going to stand against my friends. I'm not going to do it.

I'll tell you what I told God on an evening that started out like any other, but ended up being the night of the choosing. That was the night I watched a video interview with Lewes Smedes, called "There's a wideness to God's mercy."

"Dear God, I am unsure of what is right because there are people I respect on both

sides of this issue. But I cannot stand against my friends, whose faith in you in spite of how the Church has treated them has broken my heart. If I stand against them it will kill me emotionally. My heart will break. I cannot do it. Forgive me for my weakness, my fear, my unwillingness to take chances, and for all the times when I have been wrong and believed the wrong things. I pray that you bless whatever goodness you find in me. You know my heart and my desire."

There was darkness over the waters and over me for so long. There was no wideness to God's mercy in those days. I did not know the way out of the darkness, so I chose the way that seemed right to me. Having chosen, I will not turn back now. It is finally done, after all these years.

For my brothers and sisters in Christ — Dave, Brian, Carol, Dylan, Tom, Don, Jeremy, Brenda, Lou Ann, and Julie R.

http://www.soulforce.org/article/lewis-smedes-video

open communion

I don't know how many of you are out there. I have some statistics that suggest there are a lot of you. A very large number of you. I try not to think about that when I'm writing. It's hard, but I have to keep my eye on the ball. I have to pay attention to the writing and not think about the people who will read it.

But, yeah, I know there are a bunch of you. Sometimes I think about you when I'm not writing. I imagine people sitting in front of their computers, their faces aglow with a blue light. I will not be able to explain this, but somehow you feel like friends to me. My Real Live Preacher friends.

That's crazy, I know. But that's how it feels.

It's completely impossible, but it would be fun if we could all get together just once. I would reserve a huge banquet hall and fill it with round tables. The tables would be loaded down with wonderful bread. French loaves, doughnuts, fresh baguettes, cinnamon sticky buns, croissants — every kind of bread you could name. And there would be homemade jam, fresh churned butter, and honey, too. There would have to be wine, of course. Bottles and bottles of it. More than anyone has ever seen in one place. There would be other drinks. Sodas and coffee and tea. Plenty for everyone.

Children would run and play among the tables, handing out bread and getting pats on the head. After the wine had flowed, the conversation would flow as well. And just for one night we would all believe in neighbors and friendship and love.

You there. Lonely girl. Yes, I see you. Even you would come to believe. Because if you were standing around wondering where to sit, a hundred people would pull out a chair and wave you over. You would blush and your heart would pound in your chest because it feels so good to be wanted.

The buzz of a thousand conversations would throb in the air. Some people would close their eyes and sway to the ancient feeling of that sound. Listen to the Om, to the growling roll of the multitude.

After a time I would step up to a microphone. You would hear a faint, "ding ding ding," as I tapped my fork on my glass. I would be a little nervous because for the first time I would see how many of you there actually are.

Here is what I would say:

Many of us have traveled a long way to be here tonight. Some of our journeys were of the geographic sort, but others were journeys of the heart and the soul and the spirit. Some of our journeys are so personal that we never speak of them. Sometimes you have to travel a long way to find food and family. I know something about this kind of journey.

My mother and father are both from deep East Texas, from the little town of Livingston. They were the first in their families to go to college. They took their two boys far away to El Paso, and that is where we lived for a time. But once or twice a year, when the days were accomplished that we should be delivered, we packed our car and made the journey across the state to Livingston. We traveled east on the road and backwards in time. It was a long journey, and we were going home.

My brother and I were small boys. We fought and fidgeted our way across Texas. If I close my eyes, I can conjure up a jumble of images. Small gas stations. Drinking grape soda in the sun while my father stretched his legs. Spotting the glowing eyes of white-tailed deer at night. Singing little made-up songs with my brother when the pine trees that marked East Texas appeared outside the windows.

Livingston seemed forever lost in a bygone era. My parents would settle back into the routine of being children and siblings. Old ways were remembered, and everyone grabbed their partners and moved in the familiar rhythms of our family's dance.

I felt at home there, though I had never lived in Livingston. But I knew that our people were Livingston people, East Texas people, country people. The family welcomed these two confused city boys with open arms, even as they shook their heads in amazement at our tender, white feet and strange fear of fresh vegetables.

The weather was different, the smells were different, the accents and attitudes were different. But nothing was as new and unfamiliar as the food. In El Paso my mother bought our food at the grocery store. In Livingston my grandfather had a garden big enough to require a small tractor. We ate the fish he caught, the fruit he grew, and the vegetables he pulled from the ground. The fresh vegetables were strange to us at first. But in time we got used to them, and then we came to love them. It was as if this food was made for my soul. Or maybe my soul was born at my grandmother's table.

Cream Peas were my favorite. The women would shell them on the back porch while we children played and the adults talked into the night. My grandmother would cook Cream Peas with butter and a little bacon. How can I describe the taste of them? They are like the soft, light, and buttery young cousin of the harsher, Black-Eyed Pea.

The food we ate in Livingston was earthy because it had only just come from the earth. You ate the fruit of labor and land, and there were a hundred stories and traditions behind the preparing and the consuming. Country cooking is rich and fat and flavorful. It nurtures working men and women. It grows children. It makes a home.

We never forget the food of our homeland. We long for it always. I have a black, cast-iron skillet at home, and I can make corn bread if I feel a need for it. I know how to make it so that the outside is crisp and brown, but the inside is soft. I keep my eyes open for roadside stands that might sell the very rare and hard to find Cream Peas. How I long for them. Perhaps I shall have some next year in Jerusalem, or maybe in Nacogdoches.

We lived far from East Texas, but it was still home for me. In Livingston you were loved, family was close, and the food nourished your body and your soul. I never lived in East Texas, but East Texas lives in me. I cannot escape it. I will never forget it. No matter where I go or what I do, I always remember the summer nights and the laughter of the women shelling peas. I remember my people. I remember who I am and who I long to be.

So many of us have lost our sense of home over the years. Others never had a home to speak of. And that is why I say that we have journeyed long and far to be here together tonight. For those of us who are Christians, the bread and wine are symbols of something old and rich and meaningful. The bread nourishes more than our bodies, and the wine loosens more than our tongues. This meal is a celebration of the redemption we have always hoped for, always sought, and desperately needed to find. We consider ourselves to be a family in this faith.

Those of you who are not a part of our spiritual tradition are nonetheless welcome at these tables. The bread is freshly baked. The wine is rich and heady.

As you share in this meal that means so much to us, perhaps you will tell us of your own journey to find meaning and to find your place in the world.

Laugh and talk and drink and be loved. Feel at home here, for the food is good and you are among friends. Eat as much as you want. Stay as long as you like. I'll turn out the lights when everyone is gone.

That's all.

Then I would step down and you would not hear from me again, nor would you be able to find me. If you looked for me at the microphone stand, all you would find is a hat and a denim clerical shirt, folded neatly and laid over the back of a chair. I would be gone, lost among the tables, just one of the children, just another son in this human family.

The laughing and the noise would go on into the wee hours of the morning. Slowly, people would leave their new friendships and make their way to the doors. All would be comforted to have found that kindred hearts are all around us. How sad it is that we haven't taken the time to get to know each other.

Then, when no one was left and all you could hear were the crickets, one small man would turn out the lights, lock the door, and walk alone into the parking lot. He would turn his face toward his beloved stars, wipe the tears from his eyes, and say, "We did this, and we remembered You."

a religion of denial

Back in the early 90s, there was a professional man named John who had a wife and two sons. They were members of our church. The older son, Sam, was in high school, and the younger boy, Teddy, was in middle school. Both boys played football. John's wife Allison was beautiful and very involved with a number of local civic organizations. This was the life they had imagined and things were working out just as they had planned.

Then a doctor told John that he had a large, inoperable tumor in his abdomen. Chemotherapy and radiation were options, but the doctor was not overly optimistic.

We who were his church family were shocked and saddened. We prayed with John and Allison, hoping that the treatments would work and that God would grant them a miracle. But as time went by, it became clear that the treatments were not working. The tumor did not decrease in size.

The people of our church are committed to prayer. Prayer is a sacred part of our spiritual tradition, and it is an important part of our covenant with each other. Even when we do not understand what is happening, we give ourselves to the discipline of prayer. We put the best we have into it.

We are also aware that most of the time God allows things to take their natural course. When last I checked, the death rate was holding steady at 100 percent. That means that no matter how many miracles you name and claim, at some point your prayers for healing will be answered with a no.

John continued his treatments. We prayed and waited with them. At the suggestion of a friend, he and his family visited another church in a nearby city. This church, they were told, believed very strongly in healing. In fact, they believed in healing so much that they would claim their miracles ahead of time. Their conviction was that God promises health and healing in the Bible. So if your faith is strong enough, you can claim your miracle before you even receive it. This claiming was thought by the people of that church to be evidence of solid faith. Doubt, on the other hand, was evidence of a lack of faith.

I will admit there are places in the Bible that say having faith is an important part of praying. I will also tell you that these few passages should be read along with the rest of the Bible's witness on prayer, and not read in isolation with improper emphasis applied.

John and Allison were fairly desperate, as you can imagine, so they left our church and joined the church that promised miracles and healing. They weren't angry with us but this other church was saying things that gave them hope. I'm sure that after all the bad news, any hope for a healing felt good to them.

A few weeks after they joined the other church, John announced that his miracle had happened. He had been healed of his cancer. Their church celebrated, and there was even an article about it in the local newspaper titled, "I Am Healed!"

Unfortunately, John's doctor could still feel the tumor when he pressed on John's abdomen. The doctor told John that the tumor was still there, but he would hear nothing of it. At the encouragement of their church, neither John or Allison would even talk about the tumor. Nor were their boys allowed to speak of it. Even admitting the presence of the tumor might be seen by God as a lack of faith. If they wanted to receive a miracle, it was critical that they have no doubts whatsoever.

As far as I know, John boldly claimed that he had been healed right up until the day the cancer killed him.

I attended the funeral, which was held at their new church. Everyone seemed very upbeat as they celebrated John's life. Then the pastor rose to speak.

He looked down from his pulpit at John's family, and said,

"Allison, Sam, and Teddy, don't cry for John. You have no reason to cry because he's not dead. I know the doctors say he is dead. I know that everyone thinks he is dead, but he's not."

This got everyone's attention. I know I sat up a little straighter when I heard it.

Then the pastor continued,

"John is alive right now in heaven with Jesus. And because he is in heaven, he's happier now than ever before. You have no reason to cry. Smile and be happy. You'll see John again one day in heaven."

Oh, alive in heaven. You could feel the people settling back into their seats. Well, yeah, he's alive with Jesus, but he's still dead here on earth. That's why they put him in that fancy box at the front of the church.

Being with Jesus in heaven is also a part of our theology, and it certainly has a proper place in a Christian funeral, but heaven should never be used to talk people out of their grief.

I thought to myself, "My God, these boys were not allowed to talk about their father's cancer. They were not allowed to admit the reality of it. They were not allowed to prepare themselves for his death. And now that he has died, they aren't even allowed to cry because that would show a lack of faith."

Before the service ended, Allison, Sam, and Teddy rose and walked down the aisle to the back of the church. When Sam went by me, I saw his teeth were clinched and his face was rigid. His eyes were moist, but his chin was held high and his face was hard. You can tell a lot about the state of a person's soul if you look at the way his jaw is set.

I'm not a prophet nor the son of a prophet, but some wisdom is given me. I think I can tell you what happened to Sam in the months and years that followed. Sam swallowed his own grief. He squeezed it down his gullet and into his abdomen, into the place where men most often store their sorrows. He swallowed his pain because men do that and because he was told that denying his grief was a Godly thing to do. And there, in the pit of his stomach, his grief became an emotional bezoar, a knotted and tortured mass of undigested sorrow.

Religion that denies the body becomes sick and destructive. Sam has hard grief work to do because his church would not help him with it. Grief will not be denied. Sam's sorrow will remain in his belly, an invisible tumor that no doctor can feel.

And one day he will have to cough that bastard up.

the ministers morgue

I got the news that a minister friend had died in Waco. He dropped dead right on the sidewalk. There was no warning. A witness said he looked surprised for a moment, and then fell in a heap. I hadn't heard from Doug in years, so I was surprised to find that my name was in his wallet, listed as the person to contact in an emergency. He had a wife, but she left him years ago. I heard he was working at a church in Waco. I wondered why they didn't call someone in the congregation.

The police told me I needed to go to Waco to identify the body. I had never done that before, so I was a little nervous. But what choice did I have? Doug was a friend, even if we hadn't seen each other recently. He needed this last thing done for him, and apparently I was the only one to do it.

It's about a three hour drive to Waco, so I had time to think. Doug was one of the good guys. He was serious about his Christianity. He wanted to do the right thing. He'd always been honest from the pulpit and in person. I found myself wishing I hadn't lost touch with him.

The Waco city morgue looked like the basement of a hospital in the 1940s. Badly colored tile floors and shiny metal surfaces everywhere. I found the guy in charge, but he said that no one named Doug had been brought there.

"Are you sure?" I said. "The Waco police called and said his body had been taken to the morgue. He was about my age. I think he was a minister in a church here in town."

"Oh, he'll be at the Minister's Morgue. You need to go there."

"The Minister's Morgue? Never heard of it."

"Yeah, it's a special morgue at that old chapel in Waco Park. The Church maintains it, and all ministers who die suddenly are taken there."

"What do you mean, 'The Church maintains it?' What church? Is it some denominational thing?"

"Look buddy, I don't know anything about that. I just know the guys who run it wear crosses on chains around their necks. They're like spooky priests or something; I don't know. When a ministers dies kind of sudden-like—unexpected—they show up take him away. I don't know anything else about it."

I went to college in Waco, but that was many years ago. I had a vague memory of a little chapel near the back of the park, down close to the river. I wandered through the park, keeping the river in sight on my right. I found a little stone church right by the park's back fence. It wasn't much larger than a small cottage. Behind the fence was a wall of tangled and wild-looking forest. There didn't seem to be any way a building like this could be a morgue. I cautiously stuck my head in the door and called out.

"Hello. I'm looking for the Minis...some kind of morgue or something? I might be in the wrong place. Is there anyone here who can help me?"

No one answered, so I stepped inside. The chapel was beautiful. It seemed ancient, with stone walls and a stone floor. There were dark, wooden pews and a single aisle that led to a simple pulpit, also of dark wood. On the wall behind the pulpit was a stand with a few votive candles burning in it. The windows were stained glass, which let in just the right amount of light and colored it nicely. It was one of the most beautiful places I'd ever seen. If I hadn't been there to identify a body, I would have loved to have spent an hour or so in meditation and prayer.

I wandered down the aisle and inspected the candles. When I turned around I noticed a wooden door at the back of the church. There was a bronze plaque on it that said, "The Morgue."

"Holy shit!" I said out loud. "There really is a morgue here."

I slowly opened the door, a little nervous about what I might find behind it. There were stairs leading to a basement. There was light coming through the window in a door at the bottom of the stairs. It looked like fluorescent light. The light flickered a bit, so I knew someone was moving around in the room behind the door.

I descended the stairs, but before I could open the door, a man wearing surgical scrubs saw me through the window and hurried over. He came out and quickly closed the door. He put his hands behind him and leaned back against it.

"Can I help you?"

"I'm here to identify a body."

"No one is allowed in here except clergy. Are you a minister? Do you have a clergy card or some credentials?"

"Well, I'm a Baptist minister, and we don't go in much for cards and credentials. So I guess not."

"You'll have to take the test then. I'll ask you three questions, just to make sure you're a minister."

Now everything that was happening was strange. Completely insane even. But this little man at the door with his three questions seemed outrageous even in the context of everything else that was going on.

"This is like some kind of crazy Monty Python sketch," I said while trying to look into the room behind him. The man kept sliding to the side to block my view.

"Did Larry put you up to this?" I shouted at the door, "Larry, are you in there?"

"You did say you were here to identify a body, right?"

"Yes."

"He was a minister? Died suddenly? Collapsed, did he?"

"Yes."

"Well, those are the rules. Only clergy may enter. You'll have to take the test or leave."

"Okay, whatever. Just ask me the questions."

"Name any one person mentioned in the book of Hezekiah."

"There is no book of Hezekiah in the Bible."

The man seemed pleased. "Correct! That one catches most of the impostors."

"Oh, come on! Who would ever pretend to be a minister? Why would anyone do that? It's like, I don't know, pretending to be an asshole. It's not like people admire us anymore. People aren't lined up hoping to be let into some exclusive clergy club. I can't believe anyone would pose as a minister."

"People do. Do you want the next question or not?"

"Fine."

"What's a Tertium Quid?"

My mouth fell open. I was stunned. Like he hit me with a two-by-four. My mind rebooted, and for a few moments I couldn't have told him what my name was. I shook my head, as if that might clear my thinking.

"What? Who knows that anymore? I vaguely remember that from seminary, but…you…no one knows that. Are you kidding me?"

The man closed his eyes and spoke slowly. "What is…a Tertium…Quid?"

I closed my eyes and tried to remember. I was sitting in class. That phrase was on an exam. Something to do with some ancient creede or something.

"You know, it's…it's from Church history. But I can't remember. Some kind of logical problem or something? Like when a thing is something it can't be. Maybe it has something to do with the Trinity? Or else the nature of Christ? Hell, I don't know."

"That's fine. Just having heard of it is enough."

"Oh, that's nice. That's good. You're real funny. You're a riot. You are aware that I have a dead friend in there. Tertium Quid!"

"Calm down. The last question is more of a favor. Would you marry my daughter next weekend? We can't find a minister who will do it."

My head dropped so that I was suddenly looking at my shoes. A wave of despair flooded over me. "Oh God, not another wedding!"

"Okay, you're a minister. Come on in."

He opened the door and waved me inside. The room looked just like every morgue I'd ever seen on television. Sterile. A vaguely greenish light coming from somewhere. Metal sinks on one wall. Big drawers for bodies on another. In the center of the room were three shiny metal tables. The first two had bodies on them covered with sheets. The third table was empty.

The man walked over to one of the bodies and pulled back the sheet. It was Doug. He had that stiff, pale, soapy look like dead bodies do. His face, however, had a big smile on it. A perfect smile.

"Yeah, that's Doug," I said. "Wow, he's still smiling."

"Yeah, most ministers put on their smile just before they kick it. I don't know why."

Suddenly I felt very sad for Doug. It didn't seem right that I was the one who was there. He must have been very lonely to have listed me on his emergency call list. Some distant friend from the past when we were all in seminary together. We were so young and hopeful. And so naive about what church work would really be like.

"I can't believe I was the name in his wallet. I haven't seen Doug in years. It's sad to think there was no one else to call, someone closer to him or something."

"Oh, there were hundreds of names he could have listed. And any one of them would have come, I'm sure. I guess he didn't want the church people seeing him dead. They weren't that kind of friends for him, you know?"

"So, what did he die of? What killed him?"

"That's what we're about to find out."

I jerked my head hard to the right so that I was looking at him with only my left eye.

"Uh, what do you mean?"

"I'm going to do the autopsy. And you have to witness it."

"Oh, no way man. That is not happening. If I so much as see a scalpel in your hand, I'm out of here."

The man looked at me sympathetically. "I'm sorry, but those are the rules. A minister dies and another minister is summoned. And he or she has to watch the autopsy. Orders from above. No getting around it. You can leave, but then Doug will have to wait here until some other minister comes. That's why that other guy is still here. No one's come to watch his autopsy yet."

"Jesus! Are you kidding me?"

"No. Hey, it won't be that bad. And you need to see this. It's something you're supposed to see."

I winced and looked at the guy like he'd just farted.

"I'm serious. Trust me. This is Doug's last gift to the world. His last gift to one of his fellow ministers."

"You say it won't be that bad?"

"Actually, it will be. Horrible. But it's got to be done, and we might as well get it over with. The two of us."

So there I was. Just another unpleasant clergy thing. Just another something that had to be done, and I was the only one who could do it. I have learned that when these situations come up, you just take a deep breath and jump right in. I stepped toward Doug's table.

"Okay."

The man pulled the sheet off of Doug, leaving him completely naked on the metal table. He glanced over, noticed me wincing, and got a cloth to cover Doug's midsection.

"That's better," I said.

He put on some latex gloves and selected a scalpel from a tray full of shiny instruments. He placed the blade near the top of Doug's shoulder, then looked at me and said, "There won't be any blood when I cut. It's not flowing anymore. Thought that might help you."

"Yeah, thanks."

"You ready?"

"No. But go ahead."

He nodded and turned his full attention to Doug. He made an incision from each collarbone to a center point below the breastplate. Then he made a single incision down the center of Doug's abdomen, ending up with a y-shaped cut. He folded the skin flaps back, got a small saw, and began opening the ribcage. I turned away and made sounds to cover the noise.

"Ya, ya, ya, ya, ya, ya, ya, ya, ya."

The sound stopped. I looked back. The man had stopped sawing and was staring at me. I shrugged and he turned back to his work. After Doug's ribs were spread open, he looked inside for a few seconds and then motioned me over. He inclined his head toward Doug's body.

"Take a look at that."

I looked into Doug and drew back in horror. Everything was a mess. His internal organs were jumbled together with a lot of blood and goo all over the place. I don't know the details about how everything is supposed to fit together in a human body, but I have seen enough medical shows on television to have a rough idea. Even I could tell something was terribly wrong.

"My God, what happened?"

"You ask me, I'd say he exploded inside. Looks like shrapnel wounds. What a mess."

He put one gloved hand down into Doug and then the other. He began lifting things out and putting them into stainless steel trays. I watched the first few handfuls, then turned away.

"I can't look. I'm sorry. Does it count as a witness if I'm in the room but looking away?"

"Yeah, that's fine."

He worked without speaking. I leaned against the wall and tried to look anywhere but at Doug. I didn't like the sounds of things being pulled out and dropped into trays. After a few moments the noises stopped. There was a pause, and then he said, "Will ya look at that."

"What?"

"Come take a look at this."

I walked over and looked inside Doug. It wasn't so bad now that most of the stuff was out of him.

"My God, what is that?" I said.

The man stared into Doug's body and said nothing for a few moments.

"I'm not sure what to call it. I guess I'd say it's a comminuted fracture of the spine. Ever heard of that before?"

"No. But there's a lot I haven't heard of that's on the inside...of us. So that doesn't... Comminuted? Isn't that where there's some kind of... He has that of the spine?"

"It's kind of a splintered fracture. And that's unusual for the spine. Look, the spine is just a series of bones stacked on top of each other—vertebrae, right?"

I nodded because it seemed like the thing to do, and I had heard of vertebrae.

"So you can break your back—your spine—but the pieces just break apart, really. An individual vertebra can receive a comminuted fracture of course, but this is something completely different. Look here."

He pointed up and down Doug's spine. "See all that calcification?"

"I guess his spine does look a little thicker than pictures I've seen of spines."

"Yes, it's quite different. Look how the vertebrae have been fused together with this extra bone matter. His spine has become a solid, immovable unit. Very brittle. There was some kind of sudden pressure, I would guess, and it just splintered right here in the middle. See? Bone shards went everywhere. Like I said, shrapnel."

We stood silently for a few seconds. I looked up and the man was staring at me. I got the feeling he expected me to say something, but I had nothing to say. I looked back at Doug, and suddenly my head felt heavy. I saw some black dots at the edges of my peripheral vision. I felt shaky. I put one hand on the table to steady myself.

The man began to speak quickly—very business-like. "Well, that's done. Cause of death was a comminuted fracture of the spine due to unknown stress agents. The spine itself had been fused together over time by further unknown stress agents, leading to a lack of flexibility. The fracture caused massive internal injuries and bleeding, leading to the patient's demise."

He nodded at me. "You can take a seat over there by the wall. You're looking a little shaky, which is understandable. I'll close him up. We're done. You've seen what you were brought here to see."

Turtles All The Way Down

I sat in a metal folding chair against the wall while the man pulled Doug's skin back together and stitched him up. I was bouncing my heel up and down at a furious pace. My stomach was churning. Not with nausea, but with stress. I felt afraid. I felt like I had done something wrong and was caught. It was like sitting outside the principal's office. I took a deep breath, and when I exhaled, it sounded shaky. I leaned forward and put my head in my hands. After a few moments I heard the man washing his hands. He walked toward me as he dried them.

"Come into my office." He pointed to a door I hadn't noticed. I followed him inside. He sat behind the desk, and I sat in a chair facing him.

The man looked at me for a moment or two. He spun his chair around, grabbed a cup, and poured himself some coffee from a Mr. Coffee machine on the credenza behind him.

"Cup of coffee?" he asked without turning around.

"Oh, no. Thanks though."

He spun back around and opened a desk drawer. He took out a small, flask-shaped bottle of whiskey and poured a shot into his coffee. He looked at me and raised the bottle a few inches. "You sure?"

I snickered and shook my head.

"What's funny?"

"Oh, just the flask and pouring a shot of whiskey into your coffee. It's in every movie. Only I've never really actually seen anyone do it. It's like we're in a film or a story or something."

The man said nothing. He raised the cup to his lips and sipped from it.

"I find that kind of thing funny is all. That's funny to me."

"How'd you know it was whiskey?"

"Oh, I just assumed."

He made no response to this. He leaned back in his chair and drank his coffee. I thought about asking if there was a Coke machine, but that request seemed so wildly out of place that I abandoned the thought as soon as it occurred to me.

"So what did you think about that?" he asked.

"The autopsy? I don't know what to think about that. I don't know how to think about…even thinking about that. What was that? How does that happen to anyone? Fused spine? Exploding stuff? Bone shrapnel?"

"I see this sort of thing fairly often. As I said before, it's rare among the general population, but surprisingly common among clergy of a certain type. I have a pretty good idea of what happened to Doug."

"Yeah? What happened to him?"

He set his coffee cup down and leaned forward, resting his elbows on his desk.

"Do you know what a tell is?"

"A tell? Yeah, that's like in poker where your face or something gives you away. You know, like shows that you're bluffing or something."

"Right. Some people say that everyone has a tell. That's correct, but it's a vast understatement. The truth is, the entire human body is a tell. Your body always tells the truth about you. Eventually. Oh, the body will let you get away with stuff for awhile. You can overeat, smoke, lie, try to love everyone in the world, embezzle, try to act like Jesus, tell white lies for all the best reasons, cheat on your wife. Whatever. You can do these things, but the body will always tell on you in the end. The truth always comes out in the body."

Suddenly I had a very strange feeling about this guy. "Who are you? You're not just an autopsy…guy who does the autopsies, are you?"

He smiled and leaned back in his chair. "Heh heh heh. Ahhhh… You!"

I had no idea what he meant by that but decided once again not to press the question.

"What happened to our friend Doug is simply stated. He was trying to be what he could not be."

"I don't understand."

"Well, let me lay it out for you. There is the reality of who you are. It is the sum total of all that you think and feel and do. It is an undeniable reality. And there is the reality of who you hope to be, what you hope to do, the kind of person you hope to become. And hoping to become something that is better than what you are is a good and worthy thing. But it doesn't change the fact of who you are at this time. Doug was trying to be something that he was not."

"You mean he was a hypocrite?"

"Good Lord, no! Doug was perhaps the finest minister I've ever known. And I've known quite a few. His integrity was above reproach. Ironically, that was his downfall."

"I'm really having a hard time following you here."

"Look, the hypocritical ministers never have this problem. The televangelists, the con-artists, the narcissists, the ambitious. They can say one thing, do another,

Turtles All The Way Down

claim to be something else altogether, and go home and sleep like a baby. They know who they are. They've made their peace with hypocrisy. They decided long ago that they would do whatever is necessary to get what they want in life. And they usually get exactly what they want."

"Yeah, but they're not happy, right? They get the money and power, but those turn out to be hollow and meaningless."

"Oh no. They're quite happy. Delirious with happiness. Tickled pink. Glowing. Laughing. Filled with joy. Having a ball."

"Well if that's true, that just sucks!"

"Settle down now. The truth is, those people have a very shallow idea of happiness. Let them enjoy it. They live in their own world, and we're talking about a different world. Doug's problem was that he tried so very hard to be what he thought he should be. He tried be the kind of person he thought the church needed him to be. He tried to love people he could not love. And he denied loves he truly had but felt he shouldn't. That one hurt him badly—every day. He did things he did not want to do—which is fine—but he tried to make-believe that he enjoyed doing them. Worst of all, he tried to make himself believe things that he did not believe. That's the one that broke his back in the end. He tried so hard. He couldn't bear hypocrisy. You can't imagine the mind games he played trying to keep the faith. I told you that the body does not lie. The tension inside of Doug was immense. By the sheer force of his will, he developed a thick spine to try and hold it all together. But eventually the pressure was too much, and he blew. Boom."

He paused and scratched the surface of the table with his fingernail.

"They always blow in the end. You should remember that. The body always wins."

"But it seems like those things he was trying to do are all good things—most of them anyway. And it seems good to me that he wanted to be what he felt he should be."

"It was good. And Doug was a good man. But it's not a question of good or bad. It's simple reality. You are what you are. What else could you be? Perhaps it's even a good thing that Doug gave his life trying to be what he thought he should be. He helped a lot of people along the way. But just because it was a good thing doesn't mean it didn't cost him. Remember, when you break the bottle and pour nard on the feet of Jesus, that might be a good thing to do, but the bottle is still broken and the nard lost forever."

I sat back in my chair, stunned. Moments passed. The man said nothing. He just sipped his coffee and watched me.

"I don't know what to do with this new information. I never thought of ministry like this. What am I...what are we supposed to do?"

The man stood up and walked around to my chair. He laid his hand on my shoulder.

"You don't have to do anything. You came to bear witness, and so you did. You saw what you needed to see. I dare say you won't forget it either. That's all you need to know for now."

A small, red light on his desk started blinking. Both of our heads turned toward it.

"Well, that's all the time we have. That would be Reverend Sparks. He's here to identify the other body. Gordon, it's nice to meet you. Be about the Lord's work. And be well. See if you can find a way to be both."

I gasped. "The Tertium Quid!"

He smiled.

I met Sparks at the top of the stairs. He was understandably surprised to see me.

"Gordon, what are you doing here?"

"Same thing you're doing."

I watched Sparks go down to the man waiting for him. The last thing I heard before the door closed behind me was, "No credentials? Well, you'll have to take the test."

galactic pyramid

Here are some signs of spiritual enlightenment:

• The embracing of paradox.

• The love of mystery in the presence of unanswered questions.

• The acceptance of your small place in reality.

• The willingness to engage in spiritual exercises without knowing how they will work or even what it would mean for them to work.

• The increase of the love, grace, forgiveness, and patience visible in your life.

Every human being is on a journey to discover the meaning of life. You cannot avoid this journey. It is the price and the gift of self-awareness. You can be intentional about the journey. You can embrace the idea of journey, seek out paths in the spiritual wilderness, listen and learn about the journeys of fellow pilgrims, and find joy in all of the above. Or you can follow a straight path from birth to death, taking life as it comes to you and straining bits of enlightenment with the spiritual baleen that is a natural part of your psyche.

But if you are a human being—and of course you are—you will gather truth and meaning as you go. You'll put it all together in your mind and in your heart. By mind I mean the center of your intellect. By heart I mean the center of your emotions.

Here is a hard truth. The journey of every person is filled with pain. We like pain. It helps us find the edges of reality. It reminds us that we are real. We inflict pain on others, willingly and unwillingly, and if we find no pain in ourselves, we will seek it out. We will gnaw, pick, pinch, and worry the places that hurt us. Pain, like dreams, plays some unknown but essential role in our development.

Joy is also part of the journey. Along the way, some things and some people will light you up like a Christmas tree. Sometimes you will know why you feel joy. Often you will not. I want to say that you should pay close attention to what brings you joy and pain, but of course you will pay attention. How could you not?

I think the journey of enlightenment is a gift offered to creatures that are aware of their own existence. And this gift is not given very often in the universe.

Do you suppose it takes an entire galaxy to support the development of one self-aware species? It may be that only a very small percentage of worlds develop life of any kind. And of those worlds, perhaps only a small percentage will develop complex life forms, like plants and insects. And of those worlds, only a small few will develop life with any recognizable form of intelligence. And of those, a tiny fraction will develop life that is able to ponder the nature and meaning of its own existence.

You can think spatially about our relationship to our galaxy. We exist on the tip of a spiral arm of the Milky Way. Or you could use another model and consider that we sit atop a vast pyramid of life and the absence of life. The base of this pyramid stretches from one end of the galaxy to the other. Stacked beneath us are countless dead planets and other worlds arrested at some point in their development. It is impossible to comprehend the unlikely nature of our life and journey. All of these worlds were needed to produce you and me.

We have won the grandest of lotteries, and yet many of us refuse to take seriously the journey that is our birthright. Instead we sit around in the evenings watching reruns of The Simpsons, bickering over issues that will develop and conclude in the time it takes a star to wink, and picking at the scabs of our emotional wounds.

the sermon

On Monday afternoon Foy stopped by the church. Monday was his day off, but sometimes he came in anyway. He nodded at Judy who was on the phone. She smiled and raised her chin in a greeting without stopping her conversation. He went down the hall to his office, settled into his chair, and found his battered copy of the Common Lectionary.

Let's see. Proper 19, year A.

He flipped through the pages until he found the right Sunday. He scanned through the available texts. The Old Testament text was from Exodus chapter 14. He skimmed it quickly, reading parts of it aloud.

"The angel of God who was going before the Israelite army moved and went behind them; and the pillar of cloud…Then Moses stretched out his hand over the sea. The LORD drove the sea back…At the morning watch the LORD in the pillar of fire…"

Foy made a rumbling noise at the back of his throat.

Okay Paul, what have you got for me. Romans.

"Welcome those who are weak in faith, but not for the purpose of quarreling over opinions…Some believe in eating anything, while the weak eat only vegetables…Those who eat must not despise those who…"

Foy made the rumbling noise again. He reached over to a corner of his desk and picked up a Nerf football. He used two hands to spin it into a tight spiral and toss it into the air. He did this a few times, then returned to the Romans passage.

"Who are you to pass judgment?…We do not live to ourselves…For it is written, every knee shall bow…"

He let his head fall back until his hair touched his collar. His mouth popped open, and he rolled his head around a little, trying to make his neck click. He shot the Nerf football like a basketball toward his trash can. It hit the side of the can and bounced crazily around the floor. Foy groaned, long and slow and deep. Shifting forward and resting his chin in his hand, he let his gaze drift over to a stack of papers on his desk that had been growing for several months. He was avoiding the stack because he knew that if he started digging into it, going back in time through the layers like an archaeologist, he would find something he should have done but never got around to.

He took a deep breath and looked at the gospel text.

"Matthew, give me something good this week. Help me Matthew-Wan Kenobi, you're my only hope. And I do not want to fight with the text this week. I need something smooth. Something I can see."

"Then Peter came and said to him, Lord, if another member of the church sins against me, how often should I forgive? As many as seven times? Jesus said to him, Not seven times, but, I tell you, seventy times seven."

Hmm. Maybe. Yeah.

He read on.

Oh yeah, that parable about that one guy whose debt was forgiven but he didn't forgive that other guy. I can work with that.

Foy's eyes dropped to the end of the parable.

"And in anger his lord handed him over to be tortured until he would pay his entire debt. So my heavenly Father will also do to every one of you, if you do not forgive your brother or sister from your heart."

"Oh shit." Foy sighed. It had been so much easier when he was a Baptist, preaching revivals right out of seminary. Preaching whatever text he wanted.

"Well, Matthew it is. Okay Matthew, Sensei, I will let you thoroughly kick my ass all week." He put his hands in a mock Kung Fu position and made a silly, high-pitched whine.

"Hoo waaaaah"

He spoke in a deep voice, like in a badly translated martial arts movie. "But in the end I shall master you, and you shall deliver to me everything that you know."

There was a tap at the door and Judy said, "Foy, are you talking with someone in there?"

"Just having a little chat with Matt. C'mon in."

Judy peered around the corner of the door. Her eyes traveled across the room. The Nerf ball was at her feet. There was an Etch-a-Sketch on the corner of his desk. On the floor by the bookshelves was a Hungry Hungry Hippos game. It looked like someone had been playing with it.

"Who's Matt?"

Foy held up the Bible.

"You know, Matthew, Mark, Luke…Olivia, Newt, and John."

"Oh," she said, as if she understood, but she left just enough lilt in the "oh" to express her concern.

"Jenny wants you to call her," she said, as she backed out of the room.

Foy smiled. Judy had been the secretary at the church since the Han Dynasty. She didn't approve of his growing collection of toys, action figures, and other oddities that crowded his shelves.

That's as far as I need to be on a Monday. Matthew it is.

He got up and turned off the light. Looking back at the Lectionary on his desk, he raised his hand, with palm forward and index and middle fingers raised.

"And I forgive you, Matthew, for putting such a terrible ending on that passage. What WERE you thinking?"

He laughed.

"Another week of the Bible messing with my mind."

త్రం త్రం త్రం త్రం త్రం

Over the next couple of days, Foy mentally rehearsed the conversation between Jesus and the disciples.

"So how many times are we supposed to forgive? I mean, you have to admit there must be an ending point. So, I don't know, some people say like four times maybe? Seems like you want a little more than that. Maybe seven times?"

"No, no. Putting a number on it is not…that's not the way of…okay, you want a number, Peter? All right. How about seventy times seven. There you go, there's a number for you."

"What? That's like…" Peter's lips moved and he touched the fingertips of his left hand with his right index finger, one after the other. "That's like…a lot. Hundreds. Like more than 400."

"It's 490 times," said Matthew, stepping forward. "Four. Hundred. Ninety. Times. You know what that would be like? Guy punches you in the nose one morning. You say, 'Ouch, dammit that hurt.' He says, 'Oh, I'm sorry.' You say, 'S'okay, I forgive you.' The next day he does the same thing. 'Bam, ouch, sorry, I forgive you.' Next day, 'Bam, ouch, sorry, it's okay.'

"It's like eighteen months, every day. The guy starts hitting you in early summer. Every day for a year until it's summer again, and then on into late fall. You get punched in the face every day. What's that going to do for anyone?"

On Wednesday Foy looked up a couple of articles on the Internet. One was about a black woman who had thrown her body over a KKK marcher to protect him from an angry mob. The other was about a boy who was kidnapped and shot in the eye. He barely survived. As an adult he became a minister. When he found out that the man who shot him was in a local prison, he started visiting him. They eventually became friends, and he visited him in prison until the man died. Then he did the funeral.

Foy carried these things around inside of him, letting them percolate.

And then it was Thursday. Foy had arranged that on Thursdays he was not to be disturbed except for emergencies. He came in with a cup of coffee and a doughnut for Judy, as had become their Thursday tradition. After getting his messages, he said, "I'm off to see if I can find a sermon."

There was a desk in Foy's office, but he had pushed it against the wall because he didn't like sitting behind it. There was a plant in the open space where a chair would normally go. The top of the desk was covered with piles of books and papers. In the center of the room was a round table. Foy got a coffee mug filled with pencils and highlighters and sat it in the center of the table. He grabbed four or five sheets of heavy, 11x17 inch paper and put them on the table as well. Then he stood in front of his bookshelves. The books were arranged by basic subject. General scriptures and hermeneutics, Old Testament, New Testament, Church History, Ethics and Theology, Pastoral Care, Liturgical & Worship Resources, Contemplative Spirituality, World Religions, and then a large collection of dictionaries, Bibles, lexicons, and other language and subject helps.

Let's see...Bruner. He pulled the second volume of a 2-volume commentary on Matthew from the shelves. *Gundry, yes. Barclay of course. Um...*He ran his hands across the spines of the books. Turning to his collection of parable resources, he took Bernard Brandon Scott, Capon, Jeremias, and an old book by George Buttrick that he loved. He grabbed his Greek New Testament and a parsing guide, because his vocabulary had gone all to hell over the years.

Foy stacked these books on the table and returned to the shelves.

"The problem with this passage is we don't know what forgiveness even means. We don't even know what it means in English. That's going to be key. What is Matthew saying that Jesus said we should do?"

He had to move a fossil, a G.I. Joe, and a Rosie the Riveter action figure to get to his big Greek lexicon, the Arndt and Gingrich. He pulled it and laid it on the table with the other books.

Oh, what's that word?

Foy opened his Greek New Testament to Matthew 18:21.

Then came the Peter…no coming. Then coming, Peter said to him, Lord…posakis? What's posakis?

He checked his parsing guide.

Only occurs 3 times in the New Testament. No wonder. Posakis: how many times.

Then coming, Peter said to him, Lord, how many times hamartesei…uh, hamar… what's that word—oh yeah, sin. How many times sin unto me…into me… AGAINST me the brother of me and apheso. There you are—apheso, aphiemi, forgive.

Foy leaned over and grabbed the first volume of *Kittel's Theological Dictionary of the New Testament*. He had saved money for a year to buy the whole set by mail order, and he was proud of it. Ten volumes in their classic blue covers. Foy flipped to the article on aphiemi and began reading.

"To send off, richly attested in Greek from an early period…"

Whatever, just what does it mean?

"To hurl…" *Hurl!* He chuckled.

"To release, to let go, to let it be."

Foy leaned back in his chair. *So the idea behind Matthew's word is letting go. That's got promise. I can work with that.*

He flipped a few pages over in Kittel. *How are other people using aphiemi in the New Testament?*

ॐ ॐ ॐ ॐ ॐ

After lunch Foy got a pen and several nice pencils and started writing on the 11x17 paper. He wrote down the major movements of the text and made bullet points of ideas and thoughts. He got his copy of "Draw Squad" by Mark Kistler and spent fifteen minutes drawing buildings and coke cans and corked bottles floating in water. Shading was what he loved. Cross-hatch shading, shading with the side of the pencil, smudging the graphite with his finger.

He moved back and forth between drawing and writing, becoming fully engrossed in the text. At three o'clock he left the church to visit an elderly man in the hospital. Then he had a cup of coffee with someone who had visited the church and wanted to talk. Over coffee the man said that he was worried that Foy's church didn't believe the Bible enough. He felt the church would have to believe the Bible a little more before he could join the community.

⟋⟍ ⟋⟍ ⟋⟍ ⟋⟍ ⟋⟍

Friday was Judy's day off, so there was no one at the church but Foy. He walked down a darkened hall toward the sanctuary. No other kind of alone feels like being alone at church. Dark, empty churches scared Foy as a boy, and he still felt that fear when he was alone at church. Foy parted the emptiness with his body like a ship breaking ice. Passing through the foyer, he entered the sanctuary. He had his notebook computer, his sermon notes, and the Nerf football. He laid his open computer on the pulpit and spread his notes around it. He took the football, bent forward a bit, said "hup," and dropped back behind the communion table like a quarterback about to pass the ball. He bounced on his toes a couple of times and fired the football at the clock on the back wall above the center aisle. It flew in a tight spiral and hit a few feet to the right of the clock. Foy was quite adept with the Nerf football and was proud of that. He often looked for an excuse to play catch with children in the church.

"Oh yeah, Brett Favre."

He ran up the aisle and retrieved the ball.

He turned quickly and lofted a pass high into the air. His hands dropped to his sides as he stared at the ball in flight, amazed and charmed by its presence in the sanctuary. The ball arced gracefull toward the rafters, reached its peak, then dropped behind the pulpit into the choir loft. There was a muffled series of bumps as it bounced around the chairs. The room grew silent, and he could hear the ticking of the clock on the wall.

Foy put his hands in his pockets and slowly walked back down the aisle toward the front. The pews seemed filled with the souls of the departed saints from St. Alban's past, and the aisle was much like the one he had walked down as a boy in the Baptist church, when he gave his heart to Jesus. He knew no other world but this world. Knew it and hated it and feared it. And loved it.

Foy moved behind the pulpit and looked at his notes. He typed a few things into the computer, then moved from behind the pulpit and paced the stage like a stand-up comedian.

"The thing about forgiveness is, we don't know what the hell it means. We never define it. People are always saying, 'Forgive me,' or 'I forgive you,' but we don't define it. That's a problem. And it's one of two problems facing us in today's text."

Foy stopped walking and looked at the clock on the wall. He stood still.

"That's a problem. That is a problem. That is the problem."

He returned to the pulpit and spent a few minutes typing on his computer. Then he looked up and spoke again to the empty sanctuary.

"The other problem is, no sane person would ever forgive someone 490 times. And that's what seventy times seven would be. That would be like someone doing something awful to you—say, punching you in the face—and then asking for forgiveness. And of course you would forgive him, for we are commanded by Christ to do so. Then that person punches you in the face every day from now until…"

Foy checked his calendar and did some math. An astonished and pleased look came on his face.

Oh, that is so cool.

"Every day from now until the year 2000. And you would have to forgive him every single time."

Foy left the pulpit again. He went to the choir area and retrieved his football. He flipped it, spiraling, into the air as he walked back to the pulpit. He turned quickly and threw the ball out into the pews. It hit the top of one pew, bounced sideways, hit another pew, then dropped to the floor.

"No one would do that. Not you and not me. No human can forgive someone 490 times. And you know what? I don't think that's what Jesus meant. I think he was trying to make a point for Peter and the others. There is something wrong when you think of forgiveness that waytwhen you think of forgiveness as something hard that you have to do, and something that you are only going to do for a set amount of time. There is something wrong when what you really want to know is how long before you can deck the guy who has been punching you."

Foy stopped.

Ooh. Yes.

He ran to the pulpit and began typing furiously on the keyboard.

❧ ❧ ❧ ❧ ❧

The alarm went off at 4:30 am on Sunday morning. Foy was already awake, lying on his back, staring up into the darkness and listening to the gentle sound of the ceiling fan. He flopped his right arm onto the nightstand and fumbled around for the alarm clock. He turned it off and sat on the side of the bed. The familiar feeling of sorrow and dread came over him. It was a heavy feeling. He tilted his head back and relaxed his jaw so that his mouth popped open. He exhaled slowly, blowing air from his lungs with an audible sound.

He shuffled into the bathroom and got in the shower. He moved through the motions of bathing robotically, with a slack, unemotional face. He shaved, dressed, and stooped to tie the laces of his shoes. The last pull on the laces always marked a strange transition.

It's time to be thinking right. It's time to get where you need to be.

Foy stood in the door of the bathroom. Light spilled onto the lower half of the bed, where a series of lumps, like a small mountain range, led out of the light and, after some twists and turns, ended in a mass of hair pressed into a pillow. He watched Jenny in silence. She inhaled silently but exhaled in heaves, each breath like a deep sigh. Seeing her huddled in a fetal position, with her back toward the center of the bed, Foy was struck by how child-like she looked. He wondered if what she was really doing was trying to get as far away from him as possible. He quickly left the bedroom. Those thoughts weren't getting him where he needed to be.

In the dark, Foy felt his way past the living room furniture and into the kitchen. He opened the refrigerator, squinting in the sudden light. He scanned the contents, looking for something. Then he realized he wasn't hungry. He closed the refrigerator, picked up his briefcase, and left the house.

Summer was passing and the air was surprisingly cool for San Antonio. Orion was up in the early morning, along with all the winter constellations. He stared at them and felt himself relax. The stars were his silent, watching friends. Never changing. Neither his birth, nor his death, not his life, his sorrow, or his joy would move them. This was religion in its oldest and purest form. No rules. Just this reality: you are very small and insignificant. He nodded briefly at the stars, finding a strange pleasure in their total disregard of his life. This primitive act of worship helped him. It got him a little closer to where he needed to be.

"It's going to be okay," he said out loud.

As he pulled his car onto the street, he turned on the radio. One of the stations had an early morning infomercial on, advertising herbal pills that were supposed to help your joints. He listened but didn't pay much attention. He just liked the voices in the background. He drove through the dark streets until he turned into the parking lot of the church. He shut off the engine, and the voices from the radio died along with the the motor. The sound of his car door closing was so harsh in the quiet cool of early morning that he winced. His shoes crunched through loose bits of gravel and asphalt as he walked toward the church. When he stepped onto the sidewalk the sound of his footsteps grew softer. He fumbled briefly with his keys and put one into the lock of an old wooden door that opened directly into the back of the sanctuary.

The door was not used by many people, mostly by ministers coming and going before and after services. But the church was so old that even with scant use the door had become worn over the years. The wood and the hinges and the stone frame had been anchored together for so long that they seemed fused into one substance. The door was heavy. As Foy pushed it open, the smell of the old church building hit him. It was a slightly musty smell of wood, stone, aging fabric, and a thousand other things. He liked the smell; it got him another step closer to where he needed to be. For a moment he felt like a shaman priest of old, standing in the darkness amidst the pleasing odors of ancient things. The tiny glow from the Christ candle was the only visible light. It throbbed gently, casting a faint pattern on the back wall. Foy turned on a light that shone down from the rafters onto the pulpit area. He never turned on all the lights in the sanctuary at once. The idea of a sudden burst of light in this place was horrifying to him. Even this small amount of artificial light was bad. The magic was broken.

"Get busy, hired man," the lights seemed to say. "You have work to do, and you are nowhere near the place you need to be."

He walked up the center aisle toward the back of the church, looking right and left between the pews. He returned hymnals and Books of Common Prayer to their holders and picked up a few sheets of discarded paper. He checked the bathrooms in the foyer to make sure they were clean, then headed to his office to get his sermon notes. Returning to the sanctuary, he raised the dimmer switch on the lights until there was just enough light to see the pews. He stood behind the pulpit and looked out into the soft light of the room. Everything needed to be soft in the beginning. That helped him get where he needed to be. He took a deep breath and began his sermon.

"Today's text is a wonderful story from the gospels. If you've been in church for many years, you'll recognize it, of course. And like all the gospel stories, it brings out the humanity of the disciples with a wonderful and simple clarity. For they struggled with the same things we struggle with. In this case, they were wondering how many times we should forgive people who constantly hurt us.

And that is a very real question, especially for those of us who have been hurt and wounded and find ourselves both desiring love and friendship, but also afraid of the inevitable pain that comes with it."

Foy stopped and looked out at the pews, thinking intently. He bent his head and wrote something on his sermon notes. Over the next hour he spoke and wrote and walked back and forth, mumbling to himself and occasionally speaking aloud to an imaginary congregation. He worked his way through the entire sermon in this fashion. As daylight rose outside, the light in the room increased slowly. When he finished he glanced at the clock on the back wall. It read 7:55. His sorrow was gone; so was his fear. What could be done was done.

He strode purposefully back to his office and made changes to his sermon notes on the computer, printed a fresh copy, and put it between the pages of his Bible, marking the location of the text.

"It is finished," he said, with an audible sigh of relief. A smile crept onto his face. He was just about where he needed to be.

Foy sat in his office, waiting for the church people who show up early on Sundays. He breathed slowly and deliberately, enjoying the silence. The clock on his desk ticked softly. Outside he could hear cars driving by as the world came alive. He slowly lost feeling in his hands and body as he floated in a prayer-like state. He closed his right eye and held up his thumb so that it blocked his view of the clock. He opened his right eye and closed his left. His thumb jumped sideways and revealed the clock. It was 8:30. He did this a number of times, watching his thumb jump back and forth. Suddenly he stood up and ran to the sanctuary. He walked among the pews until he found his Nerf football lying on the floor where it had landed on Friday. He threw it through the open door at the back of the sanctuary.

"Yes, Johnny Unitas. Johnny U."

Foy ran up the center aisle and into the foyer. He scooped up the ball and tucked it under his arm. Dodging back and forth as he ran down the hall, he burst through the door to the office area. He feinted hard to the left and then ran by Judy's desk, swiveling his hips away, as if it were trying to tackle him. He slowed down and trotted into his office. He stood there, breathing hard and smiling. He dropped the football to the floor and sat back down. The words of the text came to him, and he spoke them aloud.

"How many times shall you forgive your brother? Not seven times, I say, but seventy times seven."

He spoke the text again, but this time the words were different, and he did not know where they came from.

"How many times can you bind the strong man and plunder his house? Seven times? No, but I say to you, seventy times seven and every Sunday morning until the end of the ages."

Foy heard the main door to the church open. There were faint voices and rustling sounds.

It's probably the Camerons.

He heard the sound of the Cameron children fighting over something. Foy grabbed a handful of hard candy from a box near his desk and stuffed it into his pocket. He walked out of the office area and around a corner. As he turned, a smile appeared on his face. He held out his arms as Hannah Cameron came running to him. She wrapped her arms around his knees and looked up. Foy pulled a piece of candy from his pocket and gave it to her. Steven was older and more subdued, but he wanted candy too. He gave Foy a hug and was rewarded with a piece.

Doris Cameron saw Foy and said, "Good morning."

Foy watched her face intently. Her greeting seemed a little forced. He knew it was hard to get children dressed and off to church, especially for a single mom.

Foy put his arms around her and gave her a respectful, sideways hug.

"I am SO glad to see you this morning," he said.

And as far as he could tell, he really was.

soft true strong and you

Children are so soft. Their skin is fragrant and pure, like baby leaves. Their minds are eager and ready, their hearts are trusting and open, and their eyes will lead you softly to the very bottom of their souls.

Children know God because God can be found in the soft places of the world. In mother's hands and in father's soft shirts. In laughter and at dinner and in the goose bumps that rise when lips slide across skin.

It is a terrible thing when soft, childish flesh meets the hard steel of religion. We cut through children like butter. In our collective unconscious there is a swishing sound. It is the sound of the swords of Herod's men rising and falling on the children of Bethlehem.

O little town of Bethlehem, how still we see thee lie.

Take a deep breath now, and free your mind. Do you remember when your spiritual softness was taken from you?

Did it happen at church

What sort of church was it? Was it a brick building in the suburbs? Was it a synagogue or a mosque or a cathedral? Was it the secret church of one man's desire, or the feral church of neglected children? Was it the cold sanctuary of science that stole your myths and left you wounded and empty and suckling at the stars? Or did you construct your own lonely chapel, like Saint Frances, barefoot and one stone at a time?

I was wounded along the way. It happens to everyone. Life is hazing. It's one big rite of passage from beginning to end. I grew tough as leather, deeply protected, calloused, and hard. But I worked my leather with the oil of my hands and with tears and time until I became soft again. And soft, worn leather is such a comfort to have and to hold.

Now I guard children's hearts against all religions, sacred and secular. I will throw myself at you, church man. Stay away from that child's mind. Let her be a pagan; let her be a skeptic, a scientist, or a saint. Let her be any or all of these, but for God's sake, let her be.

Let her be because her soul was never yours for the taking. If you lay your hands on her, she will grow hard, and still she will not be yours. But if you love her and let her and listen to her and allow her, one day she may return from the far country, fully grown and newly wise.

And soft, still soft. And strong, so strong.

my house

The exterior of my house is very pleasing to the eye. It's a modest prairie home, aging well and comforting to look at. The porch is large, with chairs and a couple of swings. Out here I am the perfect host, chatting, making people feel welcome, and carrying drinks around on a little tray. I'm very engaged in the conversations, actively listening as I move smoothly from one group to the next.

People like the outside of my house. They like my front porch. I take great pride in that.

But I don't invite many people inside my house. I need to know you pretty well before I let you see the interior, though I do have a variety of photo albums available on the porch. These contain a carefully chosen selection of photos from the various rooms inside my house. I've included a few safe but slightly intimate photos of my private rooms, so that you'll almost think you've been inside.

"Wow, these are great photos," someone on the porch says. "So intimate, so beautiful and daring."

"Thank you," I say with a big smile. "More lemonade?"

The people I allow inside are surprised to find the interior is not neat and organized like the porch. Through the front door is a large, open room that looks like a warehouse. Mounds of papers, books, and dirty plates cover tables and desks. Even some of the chairs have things stacked on them. Here and there are half-finished projects, some buried under piles of financial statements, unused calendars, and receipts. Sawdust, trash and chewed pencils cover the floor.

In the warehouse I rush back and forth in a mad panic, slapping things together, scribbling on papers and stuffing things into envelopes. A phone is cradled on my shoulder, and I shout apologies into it. These apologies are as sloppy as the room, careless and stitched together with lies and half-truths.

If I see you in my warehouse, I am deeply embarrassed and hustle you out of there as quickly as possible. I want everyone to think that things are as calm and peaceful inside as they are on my porch.

There is a door in one wall of the warehouse, secured by a huge lock, that leads to the family room, which is a secret club. Jeanene and I and the three sisters possess the only keys. Occasionally one of the girls rushes through the front door, dashes across the warehouse, and fumbles with the lock while looking over her shoulder in a panic. When the door opens, she slips inside with an audible sigh of relief.

One corner of the warehouse is more cluttered than the rest. As you approach, the mess becomes overwhelming. Then you see the hidden circular staircase that leads to a room below. Soft music, along with the scent of patchouli and rosemary, floats up the stairs. Flickering lights from the room's fireplace leap out of the hole in the floor, beckoning you to enter.

These stairs lead to my sanctuary. It is an astonishing contrast to the room above. Though well used, this room is perfectly neat and tidy. Famous paintings line the walls, and elegant wooden shelves are filled with fine leather-bound books. The couches in front of the fireplace look deliciously plush, and you catch a whiff of pipe tobacco coming from tins on the mantel.

There is a home theater in one corner with a fabulous collection of movies and music. Fountain pens, inkwells, and heavy paper sit neatly on several wooden desks. All of my writing is done in this room. Finished works are stored here in perfectly organized filing cabinets.

I'm very proud of this room. In truth, it is the room I hope most defines me.

When people visit here, I look up and acknowledge their presence, then go back to whatever I was doing. I sometimes find it difficult to engage people in my sanctuary. Indeed, I can barely hear their voices.

There is a circular hobbit-like door in one wall of the sanctuary. It leads to a different sanctuary, one I abandoned in 1984. This room is filled with juvenile literature, science fiction, a record player, and an astonishing variety of sporting equipment. The floor is shag-carpeted, the walls are plastered with 70s and 80s rock and roll posters, and beanbag chairs are scattered about. Several framed pictures of girls in prom dresses, their names carefully carved into the frames, are mounted on one wall. The colors of these photographs are fading. They were clearly hung long ago in a place of honor and with great tenderness.

Recently I entered this room for the first time in many years. I looked around a bit, smiled at the pictures of the girls, and then gasped when I saw my worn and beloved baseball mitt. I picked it up, smelled it, and took it with me when I left.

My sanctuary also holds a secret. Push a hidden lever near the fireplace, and a bookcase pops open to reveal a hidden room. There is only one person who knows how to push this lever. When she enters, her eyes sweep across the walls and shelves and then grow wide. She giggles and puts her hand over her mouth. Something on the other side of the room catches her eye. She stares at it intently. Her head tilts a little, and she squints. A smile slowly grows on her face. It is the smile of a woman who knows she is the one.

In the far wall of my hidden room is a door with wedges and spikes pounded under and around the edges. The door itself is scarred and splintered. It looks like there has been a fight over whether to open it or keep it shut. A furious pounding comes from inside. Someone wants out. Someone selfish and extremely sensual, someone rude and indulgent. Someone eager to sacrifice anything for the thrill of the moment. He craves pleasure and doesn't give a damn about anyone or anything else. He's mad as hell about being locked up, and you can hear him howling at night. One day, he swears, he will have his revenge.

Over in a corner is a heavy, wooden trap door with a black, iron ring. This leads to the caverns beneath my house. It is very difficult to open this door. It takes a lot of courage and enormous strength. You have to grab the ring and pull with all your might. Sometimes this door pops open by itself, especially at night. If you walk by and find the door open, it slams shut as soon as you approach it.

Below the trapdoor are steps leading down into the darkness. Mysterious, frightening sounds rise from below: running water, the insane laughter of demons and lunatics, grinding noises like large gears slowly turning. Sometimes you hear the groans of slaves and prisoners, apparently trapped beneath the house.

I've only gained the strength to open the trapdoor in the last ten years or so. In 2002 I began opening it regularly and going down the stairs. I bring up strange artifacts and set them on the mantle, where I puff away at my pipe and gaze at them in wonder. Sometimes I write about the things I find below. But this is hard. When you write about what's below, you cannot pass judgment. You can only describe what you have found.

So many people do not understand that.

There are many other doors in the house. Some I have opened; others I have not. There is even a mysterious hallway that leads out of the house to places unknown. I do not know this house well yet, but I explore more of it with each passing year.

These days lots of people have been stopping by my front porch. The photos are there, of course, but lately I've also been displaying things I have written. I nail them to my front door or leave them on tables beside the swings. Sometimes I look out the window and am amazed to find people reading my work, all of it. Every blessed word.

A dear friend, one who spends time with me in front of the fireplace, recently asked where God could be found in my house. I tamped tobacco into the bowl of a simple wooden pipe and considered the question.

"It has taken me many years to discover the answer to that question," I say, lighting my pipe.

"As it turns out, God can be found in every room in this house. In all of them. And I am slowly learning to be comfortable with that."

sock puppet

Here are the last two stanzas of a poem by Emily Dickinson, about snakes.

> *Several of nature's people*
> *I know, and they know me;*
> *I feel for them a transport*
> *Of cordiality;*
> *But never met this fellow,*
> *Attended or alone,*
> *Without a tighter breathing,*
> *And zero at the bone.*

Zero at the bone. Read it and know that Emily Dickinson wrote that line. She closed her eyes, swayed gently back and forth in her wooden chair, and unhooked whatever part of her mind needed to be loosed from the constricting hold of standard English usage. Then she put the words "zero at the bone" on paper, where they are as alive today as ever they were.

The first time I read those words, I took a sharp breath and froze. I didn't dare exhale. I held onto my delight like a pot smoker holding a lungful. My first coherent thought was "I could marry the woman who wrote that, SIGHT UNSEEN." If she could write zero at the bone, we'd figure out a way to make the rest of it work. Admittedly, I have a reputation for wild, passionate outbursts and bizarre notions that violate the laws of space and time, but you understand what I meant.

Apparently English was Emily Dickinson's own personal sock puppet. She slipped an entire language over her hand and used it to entertain children from her porch on Saturday afternoons.

I was one of the boys there in Amherst, playing at draughts and jackstraws until Miss Emily stole onto the back porch to entertain us. It was wondrous. It was completely unexpected. It was a revelation, and we knew that the world would never be the same again. What that woman did with one hand and a sock made us laugh and cheer. It brought joy to our hearts, right up until the moment she went back inside and left her sock lying limp on the porch steps. The other children gathered around it, whispering and pointing. One of them poked at it with a stick.

But I was different. I lifted my eyes from the sock and sought the woman herself. I caught a glimpse of her as she disappeared into the house. All I saw were her wrist and hand, but they were slender and lovely, and graceful beyond all description. And I was forever changed.

For though I was but a boy, my heart beat faster as I thought about the kind of woman who could write like that.

the fabulous gordon show

Coming soon via satellite and the internet—it's the Gordon Show!

This is the television production of the ages. Continually running for 45 seasons with a cast of millions, and every set is perfect down to the last detail. The backdrops are stunning, every prop is historically correct, and the houses are all authentic; the dressers even have socks in them.

The actors have spent their lives preparing for their roles, even those who only have walk-ons. The truck driver who drove past Gordon in scene 27-7/13-18:20 was groomed from childhood to be a truck driver for that part. He drove trucks for 25 years, immersed in the culture of the road, all so that he might be authentic for his brief appearance on the show. It's the same for all the actors on the Gordon Show. Schoolteachers, coaches, neighbors, and friends were all raised from childhood to be thoroughly prepared for their various roles.

The studio maintains several retirement communities and recreational facilities for the actors whose parts in the Gordon show are over. Occasionally they are called back for a dream scene or a memory sequence, but mostly they lounge around the pool and take advantage of the generous buffet tables.

Why look, there's Carmen, the little girl Gordon loved back in kindergarten because she could color in the lines. That was such a sweet episode, wasn't it? A real crowd pleaser. Funny how she hasn't grown. Over there by the shuffleboard is Gordon's grandmother, still smoking her Pall Malls. And there's Lance, Gordon's best friend for most of the 10th and 11th seasons. I hear the cast from last season's Colorado episode is having a reunion tonight at Bennigan's.

Yes, it's the fabulous, fantastic Gordon Show, where a neo-Ptolemaic revolution has revealed that the universe not only revolves around the earth, but also specifically around whatever point on the earth that Gordon happens to occupy. Entire galaxies have existed before recorded time only to provide one or two stars in Gordon's personal night sky.

Wait a minute! There's our star now, walking though the parking lot and toward his next scene. He waves to the crowds, nods to bit players from previous episodes, pauses to comfort weeping girlfriends from those classic 17th and 18th seasons, signing autographs throughout it all.

Oh, he's heading toward us. Hush now, for there is quiet on the set. A new scene is about to begin. A spotlight falls, making you squint. You are now on the Gordon Show; I hope you don't mind.

෯෯ ෯෯ ෯෯ ෯෯ ෯෯

The first step is admitting that this is the way you see the world. It's the only way you can see the world, for you are trapped in your brain and behind your eyes. And while you may come to believe that you are not the center of everything, your gut doesn't buy it.

So own that. Own up to it.

The second step is taking a serious look at the people around you. As it turns out, each of them is the star of his or her own show. On their shows, you are the bit player. Your name might not even make the credits. It's true, they are all stars. From this point forward, dedicate yourself to treating the people around you with the respect we normally reserve for famous people. Maybe you should even get impressions of their footprints in your sidewalk.

Now look at the animals, plants, rocks, and trees. There are no cheap copies, no storefronts, no mountains painted on a screen in the background. Every grain of sand took a million years to form. Every animal species developed painfully and slowly over millions of years to fit perfectly in its environment. Every leaf on every tree grew from a tender bud and has a fragrance and a life all its own. Once you thought the earth was here for your good pleasure, a stage upon which your life is played out. But that's not true. Our world is a beautiful and rare thing in itself. Why, there might not be another like it in the entire Milky Way.

Yes, I see it in your eyes. You are beginning to understand. It is the greatest of gifts to have been given life and allowed to live amidst such beauty, in perfect step with others and with our environment. Is it possible that a higher intelligence of some kind gave you this gift? And if so, how should you respond? If you understand these things, you have discovered Shalom, the deepest, richest, and most rare form of peace.

Quiet on the set. The spotlight is on you, and I think you have a speaking part this time. Take a deep breath and speak naturally, from the heart.

"Shalom."

turtles all the way down

Children living on the edges of time zones are the ones most aware of the arbitrary nature of timekeeping. On the Western edges, they whine about being called indoors on summer evenings when the sun is still shining. On the Eastern edges, they are rightly offended when the winter sun starts to go down at 4:30 in the afternoon.

Even the best of our adult explanations are not good enough for them. They know something is not right.

I must admit that when I contemplate leaping from today to tomorrow when crossing the International Dateline, I get a little suspicious myself. What's going on here? Who decided to divide the day into hours and the earth into zones? We slice and dice time to suit our needs. Meanwhile the sun quietly makes its way across the sky, unconcerned about how we choose to mark its passing.

Of course nowadays we live in the age of the atomic clock. No longer are we held captive by lesser timekeeping instruments made of springs or quartz. We take comfort in the knowledge that our government has very expensive clocks stored somewhere, and they keep time according to the ancient and unchanging motion of atoms. No one has ever seen an atom, mind you, but we are convinced of their existence and happy to let them keep time for us.

If you ask me, inventing the atomic clock was the easy part. All we had to do was hire a few scientists and engineers to conceive, design, and produce the darn thing.

Setting the atomic clock; that's the tricky part.

May 4th, 1952

Well gentlemen, that does it. The world's first atomic clock is now operational. We have entered a new era of timekeeping. We will never again be bound by the arbitrary and capricious machinations of clockwork gadgetry. Nor are we limited to mere 100ths of a second. The atomic clock is accurate over a period of 10,000 years to within nanoseconds.

[Enthusiastic applause]

And now it only remains to set it.

[pause]

Uh, Joe? What time you got?

I like the atomic clock and even set my own watch by it via the internet. It's just that I don't understand the nature of the reality that stands behind it. Doubtless there are scientists or chronologists who could explain all this to me, but I'd still like to know who set the first atomic clock. And who vested that person with such awesome authority?

If you're bothered by the idea that our entire system of keeping time comes down to something arbitrary, rest easy. Most everything we do or say is equally as shaky. Descartes whittled reality down to all that he felt he could know with certainty and ended up with only a five-word sentence. "I think, therefore I am."

If a person wants to base his whole life on things he can know for sure, five words can be somewhat limiting.

A story is commonly told of a scientist who had just finished giving a lecture on evolution when an elderly woman came forward to inform him that she believed the world rested on the back of a giant turtle.

The scientist asked the obvious question. "On what does the turtle stand?"

She smiled and said, "You're clever, but not clever enough to catch me. It's turtles all the way down."

You laugh, but doesn't that story have a familiar ring to it?

John: Why do you believe the Bible is the word of God?

Jane: My daddy told me it was.

John: Who told him?

Jane: His daddy.

I mean no disrespect to the Bible, but when it comes to the authority of scripture, it is most definitely mommies and daddies all the way down.

Still, if the Bible's credentials seem to disappear mysteriously into the mists of history, it stands in good company alongside our calendar, paper money and the idea that people may own land.

John: You say you own this land?

Jane: Yep.

John: How do you know you own it?

Jane: I bought it from someone.

John: Who'd he buy it from?

Jane: Someone else.

Back of everything is some kind of faith. No matter where you look, whether in science, philosophy, religion, or real estate, if you dig deep enough, you will always find turtles, all the way down.

The good news—gospel news actually—is that faith is not only inevitable, it is a gift from God. Faith is a kind of spiritual exercise for earthly children who are learning humility and worship. Faith is not a manufactured certainty, where you claim to know everything about God and mouth off about your personal relationship with Jesus Christ.

I've never really understood exactly what that "personal relationship with Jesus" stuff means anyway.

No, faith is about humility, acceptance and being at home in your skin and in your place in the scheme of things. It is not our burden to know absolute truth, which is further good news since we are not able to know it. Ours is to nurture passionate fidelity.

Faith is measured breathing in the face of uncertainty. Faith is turning your heart to faithful living when your mind has reached the end of its rope. Faith is the choice you make when you face the darkness.

Faith is a Mona Lisa smile that gently appears on your face when you peek under the tablecloth and find that once again it's turtles all the way down.

the richest man in town

A Real Live Preacher Dramatized Version.

Jesus of Nazareth was in town and the word spread quickly. Whispers moved through the marketplace and were carried on the winds of gossip and rumor. The exciting young rabbi from Galilee was in Judea, and not only in Judea, but in their own village. Soon people were moving toward the town well. Some wanted to see Jesus. Others were swept along by the inertia of the event and just wanted to see what was happening.

Everyone had heard of Jesus and of his wonderful teaching and miracles, but his outward appearance was a surprise to most of them. He was a rough and strong man who wore very simple clothing. His shoulders were broad; his laugh was deep and full; his hands were the rough instruments of a man who had known hard labor.

Even more surprising were those who were with him. His disciples, it seemed, were mostly common people. A good number of them were fishermen, or so people said. Also tradesmen and farmers. There was even a rumor that a tax collector and an ex-prostitute were among them.

Some who were at the well that day wondered how these people were able to tramp around the countryside with this man. Did they not have families? Did they not have jobs? How did they find the time? What did they do for money and food? Many were suspicious of the whole thing and stood at a distance with their arms crossed and frowns on their faces. Occasionally they leaned to the right or to the left to get a better view.

Jesus and his friends stayed at the well for the better part of the day. People came and went. Some stayed to hear him speak or tell one of his famous stories. Others hoped to receive a healing or perhaps witness one. There were a number of passionate arguments about the Torah, and the local scholars and rabbis asked him some very direct questions. His answers and opinions were offered with a bold confidence. It was clear to everyone present that Jesus was a brilliant scholar and a very charismatic man.

In the late afternoon, just as the crowds were beginning to thin, a man named Solomon ran up to Jesus, breathing hard and full of excitement. Solomon and his family were well known and loved by the local people. His father Jacob had been the richest man in town and the most popular. After he died Solomon had stepped right into his sandals, you might say. He was very generous and gave large amounts of money to the synagogue each year. He was devout in his religion, and it was known that at Passover he provided sacrificial animals to poor families who were struggling to afford them. His servants and slaves were well cared for and counted themselves lucky to have such a master.

As Solomon approached Jesus, a number of people who had been ready to leave turned instead and pressed in close around Jesus and his disciples. They were eager to see what Solomon thought of the young rabbi and, perhaps, to see what the young rabbi thought of Solomon. To everyone's surprise, Solomon dropped to one knee in front of Jesus and bowed his head. People leaned toward each other and whispered. Even the disciples of Jesus, who had been laughing and talking, grew silent and paid attention. They could tell by his clothing that Solomon was a wealthy and influential man and they sensed the respect that the people had for him.

Then Solomon spoke.

"Most favored rabbi, Jesus of Nazareth, it is such an honor for you to come to our little village. Word of your marvelous wisdom and knowledge has reached us. In particular, I have spoken with a number of scholars and scribes about the things you are reported to have said and done. It is clear that you are a man of God, perhaps even a prophet sent to Abraham's children in these hard times."

Jesus turned his head a little to one side and dipped it respectfully, keeping his eyes on Solomon who looked back at him with a bright smile. He was obviously thrilled to meet Jesus.

"I've spent a lot of time thinking about what I would like to ask you. I know you are busy, so I have only one question to ask. It is the most important question I know. I beg that you hear me and help me find the answer."

Jesus waited in silence, so Solomon continued.

"Good teacher, what must I do to find favor with God and to receive the joyous, timeless kind of life that comes with that favor?"

It was the perfect question to ask and everyone was very impressed. Of course, the townspeople expected no less from Solomon. He was known for the passion of his convictions and for the careful way that he kept the Law of Moses. He was a good man, serious and merciful and always seeking to please God.

Jesus was the only one who didn't seem impressed. Fine clothing and a good reputation meant very little to him. He had met many rich men with fancy clothes and reputations they had purchased or earned with outward shows of piety. He said nothing but only looked at Solomon, whose eyes remained focused on the ground before him. Then he laughed and said, "Why do you call ME good? You and I both know that only God is truly good. Or have you forgotten your first lessons from synagogue school?"

Jesus' disciples chuckled and exchanged knowing looks. Jesus often had a little fun at the expense of pompous rich men. They expected Solomon to be indignant. Rich men were used to deferential treatment. They were used to their questions being taken very seriously. They were certainly not accustomed to being laughed at.

But Solomon didn't move or speak. If he heard the laughing, he didn't show it. He raised his head to look at Jesus and he had the innocent face of a child. There was no pride in him. He smiled. "Honored rabbi, of course you are correct. Only God is truly good. I meant it out of respect for you. I do hope you'll answer my question, though. I have tried so hard to please God and I long to know if I am doing the right things. Sometimes I worry about my life. Sometimes I am afraid that I might be missing something important."

The smile disappeared from Jesus' face. He looked carefully at Solomon, then he nodded slowly.

"Okay, fair enough. Solomon, isn't it?"

"Yes."

Jesus bowed his head, this time lowering it until he broke eye contact and looked at the ground.

"I meet a lot of people, Solomon. And in my experience, rich men are often not seeking answers. What they want is justification for their lives. But you have asked honestly, so I will answer you with honesty. You know the commandments. Obey them. Love the Lord your God with all your heart and soul and mind and strength. Put no other god or thing before Him. Honor your parents; be faithful to your wife; do not take or desire what belongs to others; and bear only a truthful witness about your neighbors."

The crowd leaned forward, expecting more, but Jesus was apparently done.

He looked around at the people, then down at Solomon who was still on his knees. He spoke loudly enough for everyone to hear.

"That's all. You have been given the Law of Moses. Know the law and live accordingly. There are no secrets or shortcuts. There is no magic here. What was good for Moses is certainly good enough for us."

Then Jesus turned around and began speaking quietly to his disciples. Some in the crowd shrugged and turned away. A good number were a little disappointed with his response. For a famous rabbi, Jesus certainly gave ordinary answers. Everyone knew about keeping the Law of Moses.

Solomon rose to his feet and looked at the back of Jesus with a puzzled expression on his face. He turned around to leave but then he stopped. He stood motionless for a few seconds, as if he was struggling with something inside himself. Then he whirled around, walked over to Jesus and touched him lightly on the elbow. Jesus turned around and looked at him, and Solomon immediately dropped to his knee again.

"Good rabbi, uh…I mean rabbi Jesus, please allow me to talk to you for a moment longer. Certainly I know the commandments and love them. And I tell you truly that I have tried to keep them faithfully since I was a boy. I have not succeeded perfectly, of course, for I am only a sinful man. But I have given the best of myself to the Law of Moses. I'm sorry, but it doesn't seem to be enough. Something is missing."

Solomon paused, shaking his head as if he was looking for words that were hard for him to find. He was fidgeting and excited.

"You see, I love what I find in the writings of the great prophet Jeremiah. He said that someday we would all know God intimately, the youngest and the oldest of us, because the law of God would be written on our hearts and not just obeyed with our bodies.

"I…I don't know how to say this, but I want that. I want what Jeremiah wrote about, although I must admit I don't know exactly what it means. I want more. I want to go further in my love of God, but I don't know what to do next. I don't know how to make it happen."

While Solomon was speaking, Jesus' face softened and his eyes became wet with tears. He got down on his knees with Solomon and put his hand on Solomon's shoulder.

"Forgive me, Solomon. For now I see that you are a serious and genuine seeker. I see your heart, and it is a heart that loves God. And because of that I love you, my brother in faith."

Jesus stood and pulled Solomon to his feet as well. He looked deeply into his eyes, smiling. Then his head cocked a little to one side and he stroked his beard, thinking.

"Will you wait here just a moment?"

Solomon nodded.

Jesus made a motion with his hands and his disciples gathered around him. He began talking passionately to them, though no one else could hear what he was saying. Some of them turned and looked at Solomon while they listened. There was some discussion and vigorous nods of approval. When Jesus turned back to Solomon, the disciples turned as well. They all had broad smiles on their faces.

Jesus said, "Solomon, you are right. There is one thing missing from your life. And I can help you find what it is that you seek. We will be in this area for two or three more weeks. That will give you time to put your affairs in order. Then come; join us; be one of us.

"Sell your home and your possessions. You won't need them. In time you won't even want them. Give the money to the poor and find joy in that goodness. Then, when I come back through town, you will be ready, and you can go with us. I have twelve close disciples. I rather liked the number twelve—tradition, you know—but it's not that important. You can be number thirteen."

Jesus stretched his hand out toward Solomon as if he wanted to shake hands. And then he turned his hand until his palm was facing upward.

"Come, brother. Come and be set free. We eat only what comes to us, but we do not starve. We wear only simple clothing, but we are not naked or cold. And the adventures we shall have together will be rich beyond your wildest dreams. Come and be with us, my friend. Come and find food for your soul."

Solomon's mouth fell open. He stood staring at Jesus for a moment or two, saying nothing. In all of his searching, reading and praying, it had never occurred to him that he might be asked to leave his home and his comfortable life. He looked at Jesus and his friends. He could see their passion for living and their excitement at being part of something new. Certainly these were the sort of people he longed to know. For a moment he allowed himself the luxury of imagining what it would be like if he were to join them. Sleeping under the open skies, visiting towns and cities all over Judea and Galilee, soaking up the wonderful words and wisdom of Jesus of Nazareth. It seemed too good to be true. Surely it could not be possible that such a thing was his for the taking.

Then he thought of his house and his clothing and his friendships in town. He thought about his bedroom and the comfort and privacy he had there. He thought about the local food that he loved so much, and about his sister and her children. Someday he hoped to have children himself. And he thought about their synagogue with its delightful collection of scrolls and sacred writings.

And down inside he became a little afraid. He was afraid that his life would be lacking without these things that he loved. He was afraid that if he went with Jesus he might regret it later, but it would be too late because his possessions and his home would be gone.

Solomon looked at Jesus who stood there waiting with his hand outstretched. For a moment he thought he would pay any price for the chance to travel with Jesus and to learn from him. Just for a moment, before he came to his senses.

Solomon walked toward Jesus. He grasped the hand that Jesus offered in both of his own hands and shook it up and down. He was all smiles.

"Delightful and wise rabbi Jesus, how grateful I am for such a generous invitation. And I assure you that if it were at ALL possible, I would love to join you. Unfortunately, I have many responsibilities. And of course selling our family land and home is clearly out of the question."

He paused, waiting for Jesus to let him know that he understood the truth of his situation. He waited for Jesus to let him off the hook.

But Jesus said nothing. Solomon let go of Jesus' hand and took a step back. A short laugh burst from his lips.

"Well, surely you weren't serious? It would be highly irresponsible for me to…"

He faltered and looked at the gathering of men and women around Jesus. They looked back at him calmly. All he could see were fishermen, tradesmen, even the tax collector and the prostitute, those who had left their lives behind to follow the rabbi from Nazareth.

Solomon took another step backwards. He shook his head.

"No, I'm sorry, but it's just not possible. Of course I can't sell these things. I mean, people count on me to be here for them. What of my servants and their children? What of my responsibilities in the synagogue?"

Even as he spoke, a deep sadness began to form in the bottom of Solomon's soul. It was like the sadness a man feels when he realizes that the woman of his dreams was his until he let her go. It was like the sadness of discovering that a hasty decision has destroyed all hope for a wondrous joy that might have been but will never be. It was a regretful sadness, born of his cowardice, and he knew it. Solomon's voice changed and it sounded a little desperate.

"Rabbi, be reasonable. A man such as myself has many obligations. Perhaps when you're in the area I might attend some of your lectures or whatever you call them. Uh, talks or sermons, yes?"

Jesus had held his hand out for the entire time. Now he dropped it to his side. He looked at Solomon sadly and sighed.

"I'm sorry Solomon, but I don't give scheduled lectures or talks. I just can't keep a schedule, you see? I never know where I will be or what I might be doing. You just have to be there with me when it happens. It's the only way, really."

They stood looking at each other. Then Jesus lifted the palm of his right hand quickly and put it back down. It might have been a little wave or it might have been a weak shrug.

The sun was setting and people were beginning to go home. Jesus and his friends left the well and walked toward the north end of town. As they walked, Peter said, "For a moment there I thought he might do it."

Jesus shook his head. "No, he wasn't even close to coming with us. It is a very hard thing to be rich, my friends. Very hard and very dangerous. In fact, it's harder for a rich man to enter the Kingdom of Heaven than it is for a camel to pass through the eye of a needle."

"Wow!" said Thaddaeus. "It makes you wonder how ANYONE could make it." He turned around for one last look at Solomon, who was still standing by the well. "Too bad. He seemed like a nice guy."

Jesus turned with Thaddaeus and looked at Solomon in the distance. "Be comforted, Thaddaeus. Always remember that what is impossible for us is certainly possible for God."

Solomon stood by the well and watched them until they were out of sight. Then he shook his head as if he could shake away the feeling of dread that was creeping into his stomach.

"The man was completely unreasonable," he said to no one in particular. "What did he expect me to do? Really, I ask you."

Postscript:

History records what happened to Jesus and his friends. They roamed the countryside of Galilee and Judea. They had many adventures and saw many things, some good and some bad. Later, after the terrible events in Jerusalem, the friends of Jesus founded the Christian Church, carrying his teachings and wisdom around the world. Their influence stretched from the eastern edge of the Roman Empire to the mysterious lands to the west. They were the leaders of arguably the single most important and influential movement in the history of human civilization. They turned the world upside down and their words are still being read and discussed today. Their fame grew and two thousand years later their names are still the most popular names we give to our children.

As for Solomon, he lived to be a very old man. He was a good person in every way. And he died the richest man in his little Judean village.

and then there was ponybail tand

9/3/04

How is it possible that we have arrived at this final moment? For years we lived with hangaburs, peasghetti, arts and crabs, aminals, and other delightful, childish mispronunciations. Each of these had its day of glory and then passed away in its time. Now we are down to just one – "ponybail tand."

Lillian's hair is too short to ever need a ponytail band, but sometimes she wants one when she is playing one of her complex games with her stuffed animals and her little toy horses. She will burst out of her room, impatiently asking if anyone has a ponybail tand. There's something about this that reminds me of Moe Szyslak on The Simpsons, clutching the phone and desperately shouting to his bar patrons, "Is there an Al Caholic here?" while everyone laughs.

The older girls snicker behind their fingers and hand one over. She doesn't notice the giggling because her mind is still wrapped up in the drama unfolding back in her room. Love Monkey is having tea with the Big Horse, only the horse needs her tail wrapped up with a ponybail tand because it's a fancy affair and even the Valentine Doggy has been invited.

The two older sisters have been warned, on pain of immediate death, never to say it correctly in her presence. I'm afraid if she ever hears "Ponytail band," the spell will be broken and the whole family will be forced to board the ship that is even now ready to set sail upon the turbulent waters of girlish adolescence. My oldest boarded this ship a few years ago, and I will allow that she seems to be doing fine. The middle one finally released her white-knuckle grip on the railing and went aboard, though I notice with pleasure that she still has her blankie tucked under her arm.

Little Lillian holds our last lifeline, and the name of that blessed tether is "Ponybail Tand."

Gracious and loving Heavenly Father, please do not send me to Nineveh today. I'll gladly go tomorrow, or better yet, some unspecified day in the future, but not today. I will not get on the boat bound for Tarshish, but neither am I ready to leave these shores. I plan to do your bidding, eventually, but if you try to drag me onto this ship, I will make a terrible scene. I will shout and cry aloud. My fingernails will rip ugly furrows into the dock.

Today, just for today, let your servant hear again those blessed words that I love. Let me hear her say, "Ponybail Tand" just one more time. I have left ponytail bands lying in strange places in her room. I even put one around her toe one night when she was asleep in hopes that she would wake up the next morning and say, "Hey, who put this ponybail tand here?"

But she was silent. In the morning, she removed the ponytail band from her toe with a puzzled look but said nothing. I'm afraid she is suspicious. I'm afraid she has seen the older girls giggling after all and knows there is something wrong with the way she says it. The whistle is blowing and they are announcing the final boarding call. I am holding tight to my last lifeline, but I feel it growing slack in my hands.

For everything there is a season, and a time to every purpose under heaven.

A time to be born, and a time to die; a time to plant, and a time to pluck up what is planted.

A time to weep, and a time to laugh, a time to mourn, and a time to dance.

A time to cast away stones, and a time to gather stones together; a time to embrace, and a time to refrain.

A time to get, and a time to lose; a time to keep, and a time to cast away.

Ecclesiastes

~ ~ ~ ~ ~

Update 9/4/04

This afternoon Lillian was cleaning up the living room where she had been playing. I noticed a couple of ponytail bands lying on the floor. I pointed at them and said, "Hey, let's get those picked up." I paused for a moment, then added, "What are those things called again?"

She said, "Ponybail Ta...," then she gave me a coy smile and carefully articulated, "Ponytail bands."

She knows nothing of the essay I posted yesterday, nor has anyone said anything to her. She figured it out on her own.

And I, it seems, have finally arrived, vomited up onto the shore of Nineveh.

the song of myself

"What is truth?" Pilate asked Jesus. And Jesus answered him not.

One of the poems in Walt Whitman's *Leaves of Grass* is called "Song of Myself." The poem caught my attention the first time I read it, and I have contemplated its meaning many times since. Singing the song of yourself has a thrilling and dangerous appeal, like skinny-dipping or hitchhiking across the country with only twenty bucks in your pocket.

Many times I have wanted to sing the song of myself, but I've never been willing to take the time or to pay the price.

What would it take to sing the song of yourself? What would it cost you?

First, you would have to know yourself. And that is quite a thing to consider. You would have to take a long, careful look into what is deep and hidden within you. What is lurking around the corners of your mind? What memories and obsessions haunt you? What causes your glands to seize? What gets your blood moving so that your veins and arteries swell and push to the surface of your skin? What comes from your gut? What do your instincts say? Who or what speaks to you at night when the raw cuts of your home movies are shown on the screen of your mind?

Knowing yourself takes a long time, but even if you take that journey and arrive knowing yourself as well as a person can, you still might not sing the song of yourself.

What would stop you?

Cowardly fears and righteous obligations.

Because...

Singing the song of yourself means telling the truth, and the truth has a way of severing ties to people and places and things. The words are spoken and a gleaming scalpel flashes. Living cords are sliced away. There are howls of pain and then silence.

Because...

Singing the song of yourself is like removing your clothes and standing naked before the world. Clothes do not make a person; they make the image of that person. Underneath the clothing lies the vulnerability of flesh. This is my true body. This is all I was given and all I will take with me. There will be no more hiding.

Because…

Singing the song of yourself creates a flash of white-hot fire in the kiln of your life. Everything that is not you is burned away. You lose it all, all the stuff you have accumulated over the years that follows you from house to house, wailing like a wraith. It would be gone forever. Burned away.

Because…

You might lose your community. Few relationships can withstand the song of yourself. People don't want to hear your song. They don't want to hear their own song. They want to sing little love ditties filled with undefined words all the days of their lives.

So if you dare sing the song of yourself, be aware that you might be standing alone at the end of it. Maybe there is one person in the world who can bear the flames and will sing his or her song beside you. This is the person you've longed for, that you can't get enough of. The person whose voice you would recognize in a thousand voices. The one who draws you out and brings you forth. Perhaps you will find that person.

But probably not. You will probably be alone at the end of your song. The last refrain will echo back slowly, and there will be silence and solitude.

"So what would be so great about singing the song of yourself?" you ask me.

I'll tell you. Singing the song of yourself would be the closest you could come to the real truth. Descartes knew this. He knew that the only truth you can know and sing is the truth of your own existence. And maybe truth is the Siren whose song has charmed and tempted you all of your life. No one knows how you have longed for her, wanted her, pined for her, and sought her in the hard places.

When I began Real Live Preacher back in 2002, I had an insane dream of singing the song of myself. I couldn't do it then, even though I was anonymous. What held me back was your opinion of me. Within days my blog had already formed the crust of a persona, a crust that has thickened over the years.

And persona is death to the song of yourself.

Every time I sit to write, I flirt with the melody of the song of myself. I can feel the song. I can sometimes imagine the words I would lay down on paper, were I to sing it. I also count the cost. Singing the song of myself would hurt people, and that would hurt me. Truth is brutal. The cost too high, and it is getting higher every day.

So I push the edge a bit. I pull a few things out of my gut that are risky and lay them down with language that, ironically, gets its beauty more from what I left inside than from what I put on the paper.

But I tell you this ferociously and with bared teeth. The song of myself echoes in my ears every day. I'm in love with the idea of that song, though I have never even hummed it to myself.

Because I would like to write the truth about one human being. And I'm the only human I will ever truly know.

chloe and the gypsies

When a Banjara woman named Mary came to talk to our church, nine-year-old Chloe was there. Chloe had to be there. We could not miss a chance for Chloe to meet a Banjara woman, because Chloe had been praying for the Banjara for four years.

The Banjara people of India are one of three major Gypsy cultures in the world. As a very poor, low caste people, millions of Banjara live without running water or electricity. Mary told us it takes about $450 to support a Banjara pastor and family for one year. Currently there are 40 such pastors who ride bicycles from village to village, doing good and working with their people. $450 allows the family to live well and within the expectations of their culture. Many of these pastors have also used some of the money to purchase cows that produce milk which is given to the children of their villages.

Mary loves to cook, so she came to my house after worship and prepared a fabulous chicken curry meal for a number of people in our church including Chloe. We all sat around the kitchen, watching her prepare the curry according to her family recipe. We asked all sorts of questions and peered into the pots. It was like having our own cooking show.

Our church first heard of the Banjara from some Baptist missionaries who worked with the indigenous Christian churches among the Banjara. The following Sunday, five-year-old Chloe raised her hand during Sunday morning prayer request time, and asked if we might pray for the Gypsies. Chloe didn't know that Banjara was the preferred name for these people, but we knew what she meant.

We pray for pretty much anything children as us to pray for. We pray for puppies and kitties and exams and dance lessons. We once prayed for a sick hermit crab. So of course, when Chloe asked to pray for the Banjara Gypsies, we did. The next Sunday she asked again. And the Sunday after that. And the Sunday after that. It got kind of funny. Chloe would raise her hand and everyone would smile. Some of the older kids would snicker. But nothing stopped Chloe. She kept praying for the Gypsies, Sunday after Sunday. Weeks turned into months, and months turned into years. It stopped being something we even thought about. Chloe turned praying for the Gypsies into a normal part of our worship.

In the early years I worried a little about how this sounded to visitors who had no context to help them understand. A girl raises her hand and says "Pray for the Gypsies," and no one bats an eye. I tried to explain the situation to visitors a few times, but for some reason I don't have the energy for that anymore. I don't know what people think. I guess they think we pray for Gypsies.

So you can see why Chloe absolutely had to be there that day to eat lunch with Mary. She stared at Mary in wonder and awe. THIS was one of the fabled and famous Banjara Gypsies. And she was eating Banjara food. I remember thinking, "There will be no stopping this girl now."

In the early days I think Chloe was praying, in part, because it made her the center of attention for a moment. She liked the response of the congregation. That's okay. She was five, and that's how five-year-old children think. She prayed through that stage, and then prayed herself right into a meal with Mary. After that Chloe seemed to understand that the Banjara are real people.

Inspired by Chloe, the children of our church began collecting money on Sunday mornings by dropping coins and bills into a purse sewn by a Banjara woman. When they save $450, our treasurer mails a check to Mary's family, who distributes money to the Banjara pastors. Chloe's prayers turned an idea into a long-standing tradition for our children.

Meanwhile, Chloe kept raising her hand and asking us to pray for the Gypsies. In her middle school years, she went through an understandable phase where some Sundays she seemed unhappy and even a little sullen. I wondered if she regretted becoming "that girl who always prays for the Gypsies." In those days I think her reputation and the expectation of the church got her through. Once you've prayed for the Gypsies for 6 or 7 years, it's kind of hard to stop, if only because people will wait for your prayer. Prayer time comes and something seems to be missing. People sit forward and wait for it. There is a pause, then Chloe's voice: "Pray for the Gypsies." Everyone settles back and relaxes. Now we can get on with the service.

I wrote a short piece about Chloe years ago on my blog, briefly mentioning that she always asks us to pray for the Gypsies. We had a visitor to the church a year or so later who said, "Where is that girl who always prays for the Gypsies?"

I pointed at Chloe, who was walking by. His eyes moved down to the bright pink rubber boots she was wearing. He looked at me as though I might provide some answer for this.

I shrugged. "She wears pink rubber boots every Sunday and prays for Gypsies. What can I possibly know about these things or the mysterious ways of the Lord?"

Chloe prayed herself into high school. She is a beautiful young woman, and yes, she still asks to pray for the Banjara on Sundays, though she doesn't wear the pink boots anymore. She has been praying for the Banjara for 10 years. She has prayed through embarrassment about the whole thing, and now it seems kind of cool to her again. Mary and I keep in touch, and she's been back to the church to talk to us. I don't know how many $450 checks we've sent to India, but it's been quite a few. I don't know any details about the pastors our money supports. That doesn't feel like something we need to know. That's another part of God's work. Ours is to love Chloe, pray with her, and let our children drop money into the bag.

Sometimes people ask, "Why do you pray?" I find it difficult to answer that question because the question itself makes no sense to me anymore. Trying to understand that question is like trying to remember a dream in the morning. I have to remind myself that so many people think of prayer as a transaction, where you say something to God and await God's response.

Chloe prayed us beyond "Why?" years ago. I guess if someone asks why I pray, I'll just say, "Chloe." And if they ask what that means, I'll say, "You kind of had to be there."

Prayer is not a concept to discuss and debate, but a thing that is lived and breathed. Church prayers are the small stories of the church wrapped up into a living gift that is collectively exhaled to the Lord over a period of many years. Our church has many prayer-stories that are every bit as precious as Chloe's. As a pastor, I have said amen to every one of them.

For Shelby's crab
For Gage's dancing
For Lillian's bare feet.
For Cynthia's pantry hideaway.
For Adrian's drums.
For Michael's folly.

For Claud's vision.
For Ben's candy.
For Tim's tears.
For Kenny's dream.
For Steven's wounds.
For the person who keeps stealing our church's lawnmower.
For Madeline's onion hair.
For when I forget the words.
For the children on the blunket.
For George's rock.
For Chloe.

Amen

fighting over the new testament

I've been a part of the Christian Church all of my life. I've watched how things work within the faith, and I've been particularly fascinated by the ways we Christians use and abuse the New Testament.

The New Testament—the uniquely Christian part of the Bible—is a messy collection of books and letters. No one can be absolutely sure which parts are important and which parts are the cultural containers that hold the important parts. In First Timothy, Paul instructs Timothy to drink wine regularly to help with his stomach problems. It seems unlikely that this should be understood as a universal command for all Christians throughout the centuries, and I'm not aware of any church that treats that passage in such a way.

Not that a glass of wine at night isn't a splendid idea and something I might like to suggest for some of my more "intense" brothers and sisters.

So from the start, we have a collection of documents that is unclear and can be difficult to interpret and understand. That's a good thing to know before we go any further.

From what I've seen, only very serious Christians take the time to actually read the New Testament for themselves. This collection of sacred writings taxes scholars, so it is certainly a challenge for everyday people. We do the best we can, but no one can understand all of the New Testament. Even those who have read the whole thing will have forgotten most of it by the following Tuesday. The New Testament is just too much to hold in your mind.

Most Christians read selections of the New Testament, usually in a haphazard manner over a period of years. They pick out the parts that seem important or relevant to them and focus mainly on those selected scriptures. Most people are guided in this selection process by whatever Christian tradition they follow. Pentecostals from Georgia find some parts of the New Testament particularly compelling. Episcopalians in Boston might focus on other parts.

Nevertheless, we all share this in common: we pick and choose scriptures, cobbling together something we call a theology. The word theology literally means "God words," and a theology is a series of belief statements about God and Jesus and how Christians ought to live.

Now it is true that a few extraordinary Christians over the years have tried to understand and organize everything in the New Testament. Some have created great, hulking volumes of systematic theology that no average person could ever read or understand. Trying to create a systematic theology is rather like a physicist trying to come up with a unified theory of everything. It's a great idea, but so far no one has been able to pull it off in a way that satisfies everyone.

If what I've written makes you upset, please note that I'm being descriptive. I'm simply describing what I have seen. If you know of a monk-like person who sat on a pillar for 40 years, can quote the entire New Testament from memory, and has now perfectly integrated all of it into his theology and life, then your exception is duly noted.

Our little slanted, incomplete, biased, and selective theologies are the best we can do. Given how our theologies are formed, it's a constant wonder to me that people are surprised and even angered when they meet someone whose ideas about God differ from their own. I'd be more surprised if I met someone who shared my own beliefs, point by point, all the way to the end. Now that would be strange.

Oh, and there is another thing. Parts of the New Testament are just too embarrassing and otherwise inconvenient for our modern lives. We simply ignore those parts and go on about the business of creating theologies that suit us.

That last paragraph is going to get me some scorching responses. Come now, settle down. I'm only telling you what I've observed. In my experience, people either ignore or conveniently avoid reading parts of the New Testament that are inconvenient for them.

Again, the exception of your monk friend is duly noted.

Now this is important to remember: all that I've described so far is what the most serious Christians do. Your average Christian might never read the New Testament at all. He or she likely doesn't even know the names of the 27 writings that comprise our canon of scripture. These people show up at church now and again. They listen to what the minister behind the pulpit is saying and take that as gospel truth without asking any significant questions. Ironically, these are the people who are often the most dogmatic and outspoken about Christianity. Oftentimes it is these people you see waving Bibles around, shouting and screaming about how every blessed word of the Bible sprang straight from the lips of the Almighty.

Anyone who has actually slugged it out with the New Testament, reading it carefully and trying to piece together the truth about God, Jesus, and how we should live, will be so filled with humility and grace that they will probably never yell at anyone about anything, much less the Bible.

Now I'm fine with this whole process. I mean, it's not like we have a choice. This is the best we can do. So I've made my peace with the reality of the situation. And that's probably why I'm less dogmatic and picky about the details than some.

But what truly amazes me is what happens when two Christians find themselves in a dispute over some doctrinal issue or passage of scripture. Suddenly they forget how messy the New Testament is, how contradictory and convoluted parts of it can be. They forget that their own theology is a product of very selective reading.

Forgetting these things, they run back to their studies in search of verses of scripture that support their position. They pull out books and commentaries; they scan denominational pamphlets or find help online in locating these verses.

Suddenly, single verses are seen to support whole theologies. Some verse from First John now has the power to shore up an entire worldview. Some obscure phrase from Jude is thought to be the final answer on how men and women should relate to each other. And some phrase that Jesus used in a parable now means that people who disagree with you and your ideas about God will roast slowly over an open fire in the pits of Hell throughout all of eternity.

These furious exchanges of quotations are like people lobbing mortar shots at each other from trenches. Those involved only get angrier and more entrenched. I guess eventually they get tired and stop. One or perhaps both camps claim victory. No one generally learns anything constructive from these battles.

How do I know so much about this? Because I used to be right in the middle of those fights. In college and seminary, I stood on street corners, arguing and fighting with fundamentalist street preachers. I remember once dragging the Greek New Testament (I had all of one semester of Greek under my belt) down to the street corner to show a sweating, shouting evangelist an aorist verb.

He stared at the Bible for a moment, then looked back at me. Then he shouted, "Your pride will be your downfall, and you will burn forever in the LAKE OF FIIIIRE!!!!!"

I mean, what can you say to that? "Nu-uh!"

Now I'm gently sliding into middle age. I'm tired of fighting over the Bible.

Honestly, I couldn't care less about most fine points of theology. I know a little too much about how the New Testament was formed, and I know a little too much about what's in there and how hard it is to keep it straight.

I have much simpler questions for people now…

"You reading the New Testament? Trying your best to understand it?"

"Yeah."

"Are you trying to follow Jesus as a disciple, trying to understand what he said and live the way he did, where possible?"

"Yeah, I'm trying."

"MY BROTHER!"

soft technology

A question before we begin: Imagine that scientists could produce a small robot with true artificial intelligence, meaning it had the ability to make choices and feel rudimentary emotions. This robot would also need no batteries or electricity. It would power itself completely with debris found on the ground. And before this robot wore out and broke down, it would create another almost identical robot to carry on after its demise.

How much do you think something like that would be worth?

There is a dead possum on the road today. A car must have hit it and burst it open. The slick, red viscera are spilt all over the asphalt. Whenever something wet and sticky lands in dirt or grit, I don't like it. I don't like thinking about the dirt sticking to it.

Still, I can't help but stare in wonder at the soft technology that is a possum and is readily apparent in this particular one. Various tubes and sacks lie around. There are no screws or fasteners that I can see. Everything seems highly lubricated, though it's not apparent why. I see no hard edges that would rub together. The inner workings are soft and squishy, unlike the insides of human gadgets. And all the operational parts seem to have been stuffed into a hairy casing like socks and shirts into a laundry bag.

This particular possum will not be repaired, I'm afraid. The service technicians we have are very limited. They can fix broken appendages and do other minor repairs, but really, when the casing is broken open and the insides spill out, that's pretty much it. Even now the sun and the atmosphere are sucking the moisture from what's left of the opossum, drying it into something that looks disturbingly like beef jerky. This drying process makes me think that water is a significant part of the design, though I can't imagine why one would use such an unstable substance as a primary building material.

I have been told, though I haven't seen it myself, that possums are very small at the time they are activated. According to the story, they pop out of the chassis of a larger possum. I find something like that hard to believe, but that's

Turtles All The Way Down

what I hear. Take it for what it's worth.

Once they are activated, they move around on their own, sucking smaller animals and plants into a hole in the front. Some engine inside converts this matter into possum stuff and it gets bigger. At some point it stops growing but continues collecting matter to be burned internally to sustain the warmth that is required to keep its inner parts in good working order.

A certain percentage of possums are involved in the further production of their kind using the method I described before. They will produce a number of new units before they finally break down for good and are incorporated by other small, furry machines, or if left alone, slowly turn into dirt by some process that I have yet to divine. No fuss and no muss, as they say.

I suppose all of this is why I have a hard time not looking at this dead possum, though the experience isn't exactly pleasant. The soft technology behind it is so far beyond anything we have imagined. It makes our plastic-cased, computerized machines look like 19th century surgical tools in comparison.

I do not know how to think about possums. Work of art? Marvelous machine? The playful toys of some vast intelligence we call God? Should we treasure each one as a manifestation of God's glory? Should we ask forgiveness for losing our ability to see, just counting them as common?

If you and I saw a possum today, I would nudge you and we'd have a small conversation.

"Did you see that possum?"

"Yes. Amazing, aren't they?"

"Yeah. Truly amazing when you think about it."

Maybe that conversation would be our best and most appropriate response to the wonder of a possum. We would let it be known that we can still see things and know what they are.

i was only ever outside once

I was only ever outside once before, and that was after Jenny died.* But that was like a kid sneaking out at night. I stood beside the door for a few moments, trembling, then I darted back inside. I never even talked to anyone.

And I've been inside ever since. Most people in here stay away from the windows, but I'm curiously attracted to them. Right in the middle of a conversation or a ceremony, I find myself losing interest. I keep stealing glances at the window. "Mm-hmm," I say, faking interest while I look at the curtains.

I may have a spiritual form of ADD.

When I get through with my work, I run to a window. I move the curtain a little to one side and slip my face in against the glass. I watch the people outside for hours. I never get tired of it.

Here is what I've noticed about the people outside. First, there are an awful lot of them. They seem to be making out okay, too. They love their children, enjoy life, and are deeply curious, as I am, about the meaning of it all. I really like the way they walk. They seem to know where they're going. They walk like they do, anyway.

One morning in December I did something crazy. I didn't think much about it. I just got up from the window, opened the door, and went outside. I can't remember what made me do it, but it was a long time coming. I think I was going to bust open if I didn't do something.

I didn't go very far. I just stood by the door. I was proud, but scared, too. And I said the same thing to every stranger that walked by.

"Look at me! I'm outside all by myself."

Some people brushed me off. "Yeah, yeah, kid. You're outside. Terrific. Now get outa the way."

But others stopped to talk to me. A woman said, "Look, one of the little boys from inside has gotten out. Do you think they know he's out here? Maybe he's lost."

"He's cute," another woman said.

Pretty soon there was a small crowd around me. They said a lot of interesting things.

"We should take him and run away. I used to live in there, and I hated it. He would be better off with us."

"No, no. They're nice inside. My aunt lives in there. Anyway his people will come get him after a while. Does anyone have a cookie or something?"

"How do we know he's really from inside? People from inside don't come out here, do they?"

"I've been trying to get inside for years. I've been knocking on that door, but no one ever answers. Maybe I can slip inside with him if he ever goes back."

I listened to everything they were saying, and then I asked the question that I wanted to ask more than anything in the world.

"Is it true you can say anything you want out here? Anything at all?"

Everyone looked at me, aghast. They couldn't conceive of a place where you had to be careful of what you said.

"See," someone said. "I told you it's no good in there. They're not honest. You have to watch what you say."

A man named Christopher spoke up. "No, that's not true. I used to be inside. I'm kinda in and out, you might say. In some ways, they're more honest than we are. But yeah, you have to watch what you say. That's true. In other ways, it's less honest in there."

I took a deep breath and spoke a little louder. "I just want to say what I want to say for a while. Just for a while, maybe. Is that okay? Am I allowed to?"

"That's sweet," a woman said from the back. "He's adorable. Let him talk. I like hearing him."

And then a very tall man named Hugh bent way down and took me by the hand. He whispered in my ear, "You can say whatever you want out here. You can. Go ahead and have fun."

"Honest?" I said.

He nodded seriously. "Cross my heart!"

*See The Preacher's Story online at http://RealLivePreacher.com/about

tethered to christianity

I saw my father preach the other day. His hair is now white, and the skin on his face has loosened with age, but this is the same man whose face I saw above the pulpit throughout my childhood. He stood like a captain in the bow of the ship that he loves, confident that the vessel would rise and fall with his voice and break the waves of human need as it sailed to the promised land.

Emotion and energy rose in him as he warmed to his task, proclaiming the truth of his beloved gospel. All have sinned and fallen short of the glory of God, but the man Jesus Christ, somehow both human and divine, died for us all. His death and resurrection forever shattered the power of death and brings righteousness to all who believe.

There is no guile in my father or in his message. He is not ashamed of the gospel, of the stunning foolishness of its claims or of the Gordian knot of questions that inevitably follow them. He is a true believer. He cares not a whit for American culture or his status in it. His greatest desire is to hear "Well done, thou good and faithful servant" at the end of his life.

Because of this, it is hard to place my father within any group or faction or political party. The New Testament calls us to proclaim the gospel so that others may repent and turn to Christ, so he does. In that he is an evangelical. The New Testament calls us to love one another regardless of the color of our skin, so racism never gained a foothold in his life; in fact, he was always rather innocently perplexed by it. In his youth he was known as a radical or a liberal or a nigger-lover. The New Testament calls us to care for the poor and needy, so he does. As a young man, he was not above smuggling food and blankets into Juarez, Mexico, when border regulations forbade his charity. Some might say that he is a social activist, but the label has no more meaning for him than any of the others.

My father is the most single-minded, dedicated Christian I've ever known. Whatever wavering doubts he has harbored and whatever personal sins and weaknesses he has struggled with have always been safely secured and stowed away in the hold of that mighty ship he steers. What is in that hold remains a mystery, for I have not been granted access to it. It's not that he is unaware or overly ashamed of what lies within him. There's just no time to focus on such things. There are funerals to do, and sermons to preach, and the sick to visit, and churches to guide toward health. There is work to be done for Christ.

Jung would say that my father participates fully in the myth of his people. My father and other Christians would wince at that statement, but Jung understood myth in a broad sense. I would say it this way: The Christian story is my father's only story, and he lives completely in that story. People like my father move history along by living within the reality of their stories. They are immersed in the plasma of human history, swimming through it, surrounded by it, making it happen.

This is as true an accounting of my father as I can give in a single, short piece of writing. I am his son, sired by the power of his commitment, and I bear the mark of it. I will never be free from the gospel he proclaims.

But that is only half of my story. For my mother was a woman that only God could have chosen, a true match with my father. She is a born mystic, a creative soul, a muser, a thinker and a wonderer. There is a primitive love within my mother that no church or creed can tame. Her gentle, dancing spirit is the only thing that could ever cause my father to turn the wheel of the ship. He knows, somehow, that if he does not change course when she rises before him on the foam of the ocean, that both his ship and his pulpit will shatter.

He still drives his ship toward the horizon, mind you, but she makes him tack to get there.

Someday I may write about my mother, though at present I do not feel equal to that task. There is much that is unknown about her. Much that she has kept to herself through the years. But I am her son. I was nurtured with the soft music of her voice, and I see the world with her eyes. I will never be free of her vision.

I was born on their ship at a time when the waters began to change and the sky to show dark color. My father bent his back and will to the task of holding the wheel straight and true. There was no doubt in his mind that this ship would carry us all to that place over the horizon. And on this ship there was only one story to tell, the story of Jesus and the cross.

But I lingered near the rails and saw other ships on the sea. Some of them were beautiful and drew my eye and, at times, my heart. Commitment was bred strongly into me, but I simply couldn't hold onto our ship. There were too many hard questions with no good answers, too many things I felt I ought to believe but could not. In particular, I could not abide the idea that ours was the only story and that those on other vessels with other stories were bound for hell. Even as a boy I couldn't swallow that.

I disconnected from the Christian story somewhat and floated gently above our ship, though my father's tether would not let me float too far away. Rather than living within our story, I watched it from above, a floating wraith, only half present to the faith, at once liberated and broken-hearted. I was the Joseph Campbell of Christianity, in love with the story but outside of it.

High above the deck, I saw that there were even more ships on the ocean than I had imagined, and that they were good. My heart was filled with joy but also somehow broken. I loved the view, but something drew me back to our ship. I needed a story of my own. And I wanted it to be the Jesus story of my youth. And so I pulled myself, hand over hand, back down to my father's ship.

Of course there is no going back once you've lost your footing. You cannot reenter the story of your childhood once your feet have left the deck. The best I've been able to do is feed the story to others while I myself am never quite filled. I circle our story from all angles, looking for a way to be fully immersed in it again, but I have not found the way back.

I've learned to draw upon my father's commitment, which comes naturally to me. Does Christianity need me to preach? I will. Does our church need me to set up chairs and make ready for Sunday? I will be there before the sun rises. Every single week, year after year. Do I need to believe the story? Then I will find a way to believe. I will live myself into believing. I will love others until I believe. I will read the scriptures until I learn what it means to be poor enough in spirit to believe.

Do I believe the story of Jesus? Yes, in that you cannot drive me away from it; I simply won't leave. I'm having none of the darkness, even if I only live at the edge of the light. If belief is a hard and complex thing, also a unique and personal thing, then yes: I believe.

I have been comforted by gentle and faithful brothers and sisters in Christ who have always made a place for me in the community of the friends of Jesus. And I believe that the New Testament defines faith and belief broadly enough to include even me.

Turtles All The Way Down

The Gospel of Mark tells the story of a man who wanted Jesus to heal his son. Jesus asked him if he believed. He boldly said, "Yes." And then, his faith faltering, he cried out, "Help my unbelief."

That man is my patron saint.

story, redemption, and time

I have a friend who is 73 years old. He told me that his grandmother ran away from home when she was 16. She walked down a country lane in Tennessee. There was a black car, she later said. A man got out and raped her in the bushes by the side of the road. She stumbled home and told no one for fear that she would get in trouble. But months later her belly began to swell. She told the truth when she had to. Some people believed her. Others didn't. Nine months later his father was born.

"That was in the year 19 and eight," he said.

I thought about this for a few moments and felt pretty overwhelmed by the revelation. His life, it seemed, was held together by a ragged thread of evil wound through a series of long shots. Like rolling snake eyes six times in a row. Why did she choose that day to leave? Why that hour? Why that lane and not another?

"If she hadn't run away from home and had that happen, you wouldn't have been born."

He snapped his chin down to his chest and bounced it quickly up again. It's a gesture I've seen old men make when something is said that is surely true.

"That's right," he said. "That's exactly right. Not me, not my children, not my 12 grandchildren, nor the five great-grand-babies."

"So..." I left a long pause to soften the question that was coming. "Would you say that you're glad it happened? I mean, surely you're glad to be alive."

"I don't rightly think it's a fair question," he said. "The past is dead and gone and all that pain with it. A pile of manure might be lucky enough to have a flower grow out of it, but that doesn't change its basic nature."

I ran the tops of two fingers underneath my chin against the grain of my whiskers. I felt the stubble grab at my skin and heard the rasping sound. It's something I do when I'm thinking.

"I don't know how things were for her. My father didn't tell me much about that. I know it was hard for him. He was either the bastard son of a rapist or the bastard son of a ruined girl. Whatever people thought, none of it was good. And folks wasn't nearly as kind about them things back then. Sometimes you hear people say how the world has gotten meaner and people are less kind today."

He shook his head.

"Theys lots of ways that people are much kinder now. About children such as my father, for example. Nobody blames the children anymore, but they used to. Kindly looked at them funny all their life. Most of them would end up leaving those parts and their people and start somewhere fresh. That's what my daddy did. Brought his mother with him and came to Texas. He got married over in Bastrop. We still got family there. He lived a respectable life. Was a good man. Course, by the time us kids were born, it wasn't nothin but an old story no one remembered. I only know it cause my daddy told me when I was older. He thought I ought to know it for some reason."

He pulled a handkerchief out of his back pocket, blew his nose loudly, glanced at what he had deposited into the cloth, then folded it up and put it back in his pocket.

"There ain't much of it left now. She's dead. He's dead. The man with the black car is surely dead. The only thing left is a story in an old man's mind. And I think I'll let it die with me. The story is dried up. All the pain is gone. I see no call to tell the children about it. So I think I'll just take it with me."

"Only you told me," I observed. "So now I know it."

He smiled. "Yeah, but you aren't family. With you it's like pushing a caboose down a side track with a dead end in the woods. It's just a story to you."

He laughed.

"Just another one of all those stories you got in your head, all that writin you do."

I smiled and nodded and got to working my fingers under my chin again.

"No sir." he said. "The blood of Jesus and good living covered those sins long ago."

I nodded very deliberately, the way men do when they agree and there's nothing left to be said.

It seems to me that every act of evil is a cosmic event, a kind of big bang unto itself. There is the moment of evil, a moment so filled with dark energy and pain that no one can stand to look at it. It explodes and sends its ugliness out in every direction. Sometimes evil begets evil, and sometimes good people snuff it out.

There was a moment in time back in 19 and eight. It was a thing no one wants to look at or remember. A man in a black car grabbed a girl and dragged her into the bushes. There was the reality of his lust and anger. There was the reality of her panicked fear and pathetic cries for help and mercy. No one heard her. Her clothing was torn and her flesh abraded on the rough earth. And God help us all, there was the raw biology of the act itself.

That is a moment that no one wants to see. Everyone turns their face away in horror. It is like an explosion of pain and suffering.

Then the camera of time pulls away from the scene—mercifully we think— and we can look back again. There she is, running down the lane, bloodied and weeping. There she is confessing the truth and falling into her mother's arms. There are the gossiping neighbors. There is the sorrow and the beauty of his birth. There are the stares and the shunning he was too young to understand. There is his anger and determination when he figured it all out. There they are, packing their things and leaving for Texas.

The camera draws back faster now. We see his joy at meeting a girl who did not know his history. Their courtship, their wedding. His mother weeping with joy and saying to herself, "I endured it for him." Her death, we hope a gentle one. His children and grandchildren. His aging face and hands. His last telling of the story to his oldest son, bequeathing it because he was not the one to decide when to bury it.

For years the story lived like a wraith in the mind of a happy and good man. His father loved him and taught him, and he made good. And now the story is severed from the family and lives in me. It lives only in these words between you and me with no power to hurt but only to bear witness as a testimony to how things sometimes happen.

For this is the power of evil and the power of goodness and the power of stories and the power of redemption and the power of time.

grit and gravel

An angel came to me while I was laboring at prayer. Yes, laboring. That is likely a problem itself, but we'll leave that for another day. I was in the woods near the church, fingering my way through my rosary. Ten beads for the Shema, ten for people in our church, ten for this, ten for that. My mind was filled with the numerous categories of language. People placed into one group or another. Actions lumped together and called by a single name. Everything classified not only by type, but also called sacred or secular, good or evil. Joy, pleasure, pain, heaven, hell, things done and things left undone. All of these were in my mind.

While I worked my way from bead to bead I noticed, with a start, that an angel was sitting across from me. It looked at me with a pleasant smile. I stood up, respectfully.

"Greetings," the angel said.

What exactly do you say to angel? Is there a protocol for this?

Not knowing what to say, I said nothing at all.

"Mortal, scoop up a handful of what covers that path."

I reached to the earth, eyes still on the angel, and grabbed at whatever lay at my feet.

"Now open your palm and blow on it."

I did, and an assortment of leaves and bits of plants floated away.

"What would you call what is left in your hand?"

"Grit maybe? Gravel?"

"Grit and gravel?" the angel said indignantly. "Each particle in your hand has a unique history, and all of their histories are older than the oldest memories of humankind. Each one has a name. Did you know that?"

I brought my palm close to my eyes to look at what lay there. Wanting to say something in keeping with the angel's attitude toward my handful of gravel, I said, "The pinkish one is nice."

"Sit down, mortal, and I will tell you a truth."

I sat on the ground and looked up at the angel.

"What need has God for categories? Why sort and catalog a collection when you know and can describe every individual item? What meaning do your base labels have for a higher mind? You have created categories for your own use, fallen in love with sorting them, and made a god of the whole affair. This is an idolatry of the highest order. It is a blasphemy so bold as to cause angels to tremble. 'The mind of The Almighty,' you say, 'is like unto my own mind.'"

"God is on intimate terms with the simple matter of earth, yet you dare label people instead of trying to know them. Your precious divisions of nationality, of Christian and non-Christian, saved and damned good and evil, slave and free. These convenient memory aids might have served you well when you were biting spiritual ankles and wrestling with your primers. Will you not set them aside even now?"

"For the Lord God, the Mysterious, the Creator of all things, is one who knows the hearts of people. And when time draws to a close, there will be no labels or records. There will be no flags, no Bibles, no creeds, no clothing, no wealth or distinction. There will be nothing but vision, straight and true. A mind that will peer into your heart and know you inside and out."

"There will be no hiding on that day."

"What should I do?" I asked.

The angel smiled. "In truth, you are a human being and can be no more than that. Labels and categories are all that you know. Go in peace and understand the world in the ways you can. But know this greater truth. And knowing it, let humility settle upon you like the gentle aging of a righteous man."

In 2003, as I was making my decision about where I stood as a pastor on the issue of the Church and homosexuality, I wrote an essay on this subject. I was very angry at the time. I was also anonymous and felt free to push the envelope a bit. I probably wouldn't have had the courage to be as honest if my name had been on it.

Later, when people found out my name, that piece was out there. It was later published in my first book. The original piece is still online at my blog.

http://reallivepreacher.com/homosexuality

Following that post, I received dozens of emails asking me to explain my views of the scripture passages that address homosexuality. So I posted a follow-up piece called "A Look at the Bible and Homosexuality." It was not included in my first book because it's more of an information piece and not in keeping with my style as a writer of essays and short stories.

However, these two pieces together have been read as much as anything I've written. So I thought I'd include the follow-up piece in this book.

a look at the bible and homosexuality

After my passionate post on the subject of homosexuality, I've received numerous emails asking me to clearly state my interpretation of the parts of the Bible that are thought to speak to the issue of homosexuality. Initially I thought I would respond by email to those wanting to discuss the Bible, but the number of emails was overwhelming so I thought I would post my thoughts here.

I'd like to speak to this issue in four parts.

Part One—Hypocrisy

If we Christians were honest, we would admit that we do not abide by all the commandments of scripture ourselves. I don't mean that we try and fail. I mean we deliberately choose to ignore scriptures that are not convenient for our lifestyles. The amount of scripture that is ignored, scorned, and abused by modern Christians is incredible. This blatant disregard for scripture never seems to bother church people when the issues at hand have to do with their own sins. But suddenly, when the subject of homosexuality comes up, everyone becomes a biblical literalist. The hypocrisy of this is appalling.

I think we should afford our homosexual brothers and sisters the same luxury we claim for ourselves. If we plan to ignore whatever scriptures threaten our lifestyles, perhaps we should offer them space at our bonfire to burn their little handful of scriptures as we burn the Bible chapter and verse.

We should all agree that none of us are able or willing to follow all the teachings of scripture. Let the one who is obeying God's word ask for detailed scriptural explanations from others.

In my book, that settles the argument, and there is no reason to go further. However, if you are determined to hold homosexuals to a higher standard, demanding detailed explanations of why they do not obey minor parts of the Bible while all of Christendom tramples on the very heart of scripture, move on to part two.

Part Two—The Bible and homosexuality

The Bible never addresses the subject of homosexuality as an orientation. The idea of sexual identity was not a part of human thought until very recently. The Bible addresses some specific homosexual acts in very specific contexts. The idea of two people in a loving, committed homosexual relationship was not understood in the ancient Hebrew world and is not a subject in the Bible. Very credible biblical scholars treat the passages in question as specific commands against specific acts, and not as a wholesale prohibition on a homosexual orientation.

For many people, understanding this obvious limitation of the Bible is all that is needed. The Bible does not address the broad subject of sexual orientation because it was written before that was an issue. Any specific condemnation of homosexual acts must be seen as just that – a specific condemnation of an act in a specific context.

However, if that sounds too wishy-washy to you, if it sounds too slippery and subjective, let me now speak to all six of the passages in the Bible that are thought by some people to address the issue of homosexuality.

Part Three—Exegesis

There are exactly six scriptures that are thought to address homosexuality. I'll either quote the passage or provide a link so that you can read it.

The story of the destruction of Sodom – Genesis 19:1–29. If you read this story, you'll quickly see that the men of the city of Sodom wanted to commit a brutal, homosexual rape. We simply cannot condemn a sexual orientation because of a rape. There is a heterosexual rape described in the next passage we will examine together. Shall we condemn heterosexuality because of this rape?

Any reasonable person will understand that this passage has nothing to say about loving, consensual homosexual relationships.

Judges 19:1–30 is a sad story of human evil of the type that is often recounted in scripture. It is basically a retelling of the Sodom story in a different context. This time, however, the men actually did rape a woman. This passage speaks to the need for God's love in a brutal world. It has no bearing on the question of homosexual orientation for the same reason that the Sodom story is not applicable. Both of these stories condemn ignorance and sexual brutality, but not homosexuality.

Texts three and four are both in Leviticus and make up a part of the Old Testament Levitical code.

Leviticus 18:22—Do not lie with a man as one lies with a woman; that is detestable.

Leviticus 20:13—If a man lies with a man as one lies with a woman, both of them have done what is detestable. They must be put to death; their blood will be on their own heads.

The code of rules and behaviors in Leviticus does not apply to Christians. The book of Acts, specifically chapter 15, makes it clear that gentile Christians are not required to keep all of the Mosaic laws. No Christian group I know demands full compliance with this ancient code of behavior. If we did we would have to keep kosher laws. We don't even demand compliance with the sexual laws in Leviticus. If we did, we would allow polygamy, which is lawful in Leviticus. Unless you are prepared to obey all the laws in Leviticus, you cannot blame the homosexual for not feeling bound to obey all of them. To point to these two verses and demand selective compliance is ludicrous.

The Old Testament really has nothing specific to say to Christians about homosexuality. We turn now to the New Testament.

Jesus had nothing to say on the subject of homosexuality. His absence of comment does not support or condemn homosexuality. Jesus was Jewish, kept the Law of Moses, and mainly dealt with Jewish people. The issue of homosexuality was not relevant or important to his ministry. It's not surprising that Jesus never addressed what was not an issue for his culture.

Paul, who lived in the gentile world and dealt with gentiles, discusses specific homosexual acts twice. These passages are the only two times homosexual behavior is mentioned in the New Testament. Let me repeat that because it is important. The two passages I am about to discuss comprise the total New Testament witness on the subject of homosexuality.

I Corinthians 6:9—Do you not know that the wicked will not inherit the kingdom of God? Do not be deceived: Neither the sexually immoral nor idolaters nor adulterers nor male prostitutes nor homosexual offenders. (NIV)

"Male prostitutes" and "homosexual offenders." Can someone explain to me why we would condemn an entire orientation because of the prohibition of these very specific behaviors?

The Greek words Paul used in this passage include the word for a young, effeminate male prostitute and the word for the older man who paid to have sex with him. Admittedly, there is some disagreement over how these words should be translated, but let me point out that I'm quoting from the New International Version, arguably the most conservative modern translation available. You may disagree with this translation, but you cannot dismiss it as ridiculous. The scholars who worked on the NIV are not lightweights. And uncertainty and ambiguity in translation is only a further argument for tolerance.

We can acknowledge that the New Testament condemns prostitution and a system where a younger man makes his living committing sex acts for money with older men. But we cannot condemn homosexuality in general because homosexual prostitution was condemned. Paul condemns many heterosexual acts in his writings, even in this very verse, yet we do not condemn heterosexuality.

Romans 1:18–29 is the last passage we shall look at. It is the one most often quoted, and it is clearly the closest thing we find to condemnation in the New Testament. Verse 27 is the most specific verse.

I simply ask you to read this entire passage with an open mind. In it, Paul says that those who reject God will be given over to "shameful lusts." They will engage in many acts that are not pleasing to God. Men will "burn with lust for one another."

In Paul's experience, the only homosexuality he knew was that practiced in the non-Jewish world and probably tied to pagan temple worship. He claims that homosexuality is one of the punishments for those who reject God. But what are we to do with gentle and committed Christians who love God and worship God, but who tell us that they have a homosexual orientation?

My homosexual friends who are Christians are not haters of God. They have not rejected the Creator. Nor do not burn in lust for each other and run around committing scandalous acts. They are quietly committed to their partners in love. The dilemma here is that the homosexual Christians I know just do not fit the picture Paul gives us in Romans.

I'll be honest—I don't know exactly what Paul meant by this passage. I know he was describing people who chose not to worship God and then "burned with lust for other men." I don't know exactly what he meant, but I know this DOES NOT describe the homosexual Christians I know, who love God with great passion.

Because of my inability to make clear sense of these passages, I am willing to allow a person's sexual orientation to be between him or her and God. I am willing to take a chance and err on the side of compassion and inclusion.

And consider this: Jesus condemned divorce several times in the gospels. You can read one instance in Mark 10:1–11. Jesus is clearly saying that just because a judge on earth grants a divorce does not mean that God sets aside the commitment. So, according to Jesus, when divorced people remarry they are living in a constant and willful state of adultery. And yet, why is it we have no problem with divorced and remarried people in the church? I believe this is because the divorced people are our friends and church members. So we are willing to look at their lives with grace and include them in our communities. We don't understand what Jesus meant exactly, but we assume they are doing the best they can in a difficult situation. "And surely Jesus couldn't have meant that they spend the rest of their lives alone," we say to ourselves. We don't offer the same grace to homosexuals because it is convenient to sacrifice them on our altar of biblical fidelity. We can reject them and claim our actions as examples of how much we respect the scriptures.

This even though the New Testament witness on divorce is MUCH clearer and comes right from the mouth of Jesus.

It's hypocrisy, plain and simple.

Part Four—Conclusion

Those are the six passages in the Bible that are thought to address the subject of homosexuality. The Old Testament passages amount to nothing and the two New Testament passages are ambiguous at best and highly open to interpretation.

I do not think the Bible teaches that every expression of homosexual love is sinful. The scriptural witness on this subject is shaky at best.

Even if you do not buy my claim that we have no right to demand specific explanation of scriptures from homosexuals, since we don't provide similar explanations for the hundreds of passages we blatantly ignore…

Even if you do not agree that the Bible never really addresses the subject of homosexuality as a sexual orientation…

Even if you reject my biblical analysis and decide that the Bible is condemning of homosexuals…

Would you at least agree that the passages are ambiguous and open to many interpretations? Would you at least agree that others may responsibly interpret them and not agree with you?

If you could at least acknowledge that those of us who disagree with your interpretation are nonetheless serious-minded people who read the scriptures carefully and want to follow them, then perhaps you would be willing to err on the side of compassion. Perhaps you would be willing to open your churches to our homosexual brothers and sisters, trusting them to read the Bible just as you do, with love and hoping for Grace from God.

de nada

Years later, he would wonder why he decided to go to Mardi Gras in the first place. He never did come up with any complicated or insightful reasons. It seemed like he went because he wasn't a minister anymore, and he could go if he wanted to. None of the ministers Foy knew ever went to Mardi Gras or any place where people got drunk and acted crazy.

He was standing outside his church on his last day, and he remembered that Mardi Gras was about to begin. He imagined himself walking down the streets of the French Quarter at night, with people all around him laughing and drinking and having a good time. He wanted to sit at an outdoor café, smoking a cigar while he watched people walk up and down the street. Foy didn't smoke cigars, but he thought he might start in New Orleans.

He decided to take a bus because of *Midnight Cowboy*. He loved the bus scenes in that movie. Not so much the one where Joe Buck rode the bus from Texas to New York, but the one at the end, where he threw away his cowboy clothes and rode the bus to Florida with his dying friend, Ratso Rizzo. People in the movies were always taking a bus somewhere, especially when important stuff was happening in their lives.

Foy put some books and his MP3 player into a knapsack, then packed a change of pants and several shirts into an old duffel bag. He wanted to travel light. When he thought about traveling, he remembered his wife's luggage and all the kids' stuff, and how he used to pack a lot of nice clothes if he was going to do a wedding or a funeral. There was so much stuff, and he couldn't bear thinking about it. He just wanted everything to be neat and tidy and in one bag.

He zipped up the duffel bag the night before the trip and tossed it over by the door. "One bag," he said out loud. "I don't know what all the fuss was about. A person doesn't need all that much."

One of the deacons who liked him and wished he hadn't quit or been fired (whichever it was) drove him downtown to the San Antonio bus station. He was very amused that Foy was taking a bus, and he joked about it. They shook hands and Foy said, "I'll see you when I see you."

It was his first time in a bus station, though he had seen plenty of them in movies. He was fascinated by the mix of humanity he saw there. *These are the people who take buses. They know what they're doing.*

Most of them were Mexican families headed south to cross the border at Laredo. They sat on the floor among piles of luggage, eating tamales and tacos wrapped in tinfoil. Homeless men straggled in and out with plastic grocery bags dangling from their arms. There were a number of older men who looked like they had been at a World War II veteran's convention. They wore blue baseball caps bearing the names of various ships or veterans organizations. Several young Hispanic men slouched on the benches in starched clothing and dark sunglasses. Their heads bobbed up and down to the slight buzz of Tejano music leaking from their headphones.

Foy wore jeans, tennis shoes, and an unadorned beige T-shirt. He didn't like words on his T-shirts and went to some trouble to find plain ones. No one even looked at him. It was like he was invisible.

It turned out there was a considerable wait for the bus due to a delay near San Angelo, so Foy stepped outside to find something to eat. Across the street was a cheap BBQ stand that seemed popular with the bus crowd. There were people sitting on the sidewalk with their luggage, eating BBQ sandwiches and sipping beer from bottles. He let his eyes drift to the left, and he spotted a sandwich shop a little ways down the street. Foy chose the sandwich shop. He had a Muffaletta with extra olives and a Diet Coke while he sat at the window, happily watching the people stream back and forth from the BBQ stand to the bus station.

When it was time for the bus to leave, Foy threw his duffel bag into the cargo area and found a seat by a window. He put his knapsack in the aisle seat and hoped no one would sit there. He needed to check something before he could relax, so he peeked inside the knapsack and saw that his books and MP3 player were there. Satisfied, he leaned his head against the window and stared out, waiting for the bus to depart.

In that moment, with the business of travel out of his mind, he began to feel wrong—like the trip wasn't going to work. Like going to Mardis Gras wasn't going to make him feel better. He recognized the early tinge of sadness that signals a coming depression. He shook his head angrily and whispered, "No!" Exhaling loudly, he turned his attention to a young Hispanic woman trying to settle herself and her two small children into their seats. She was a bundle of energy, somehow holding her baby on one hip while she helped her young son into the seat by the window. Her arms were full of bags and toys. The baby was fussing, and the little boy began hanging over the back of the seat, picking his nose and staring at the woman behind him, who was pretending not to notice.

Foy stared at the young mother, fascinated and amazed. She would never be done. The children would cry and squirm and need to be fed and changed and comforted every waking moment of the entire journey. Meanwhile, he would be indulging himself with reading and music and by staring out the window at the passing scenery, a thing he loved to do. While the woman fished around in the diaper bag for something, the little boy began licking the window with long, careful tongue strokes that left a blurry film on the glass. He was very methodical, as if he was trying to cover as much of the glass as possible before his mother noticed him.

"Oh my God," Foy whispered. "Thank you Jesus for letting me not be her."

His spirits lifted a little. However bad things were, at least he wasn't taking care of small children on a bus trip. And he didn't have to care about the woman with the children, either. She was not his to care for. He didn't have to care about her or anyone else. He could smile at the woman, mildly empathetic, across a vast emotional chasm.

Just then the woman spotted the boy licking the window and shouted at him in Spanish. She lunged toward him and a bottle fell out of the diaper bag, rolling down the aisle until it stopped near Foy's seat. He started to retrieve it for her, then stopped himself. *Someone else can get it.*

But he couldn't keep his eyes off the bottle. He kept looking at it and wondering if anyone else would notice. No one did. The other passengers seemed oblivious to anything happening beyond their own seats. Foy wondered how they did that. He was always looking at the people around him. He noticed everything.

He felt an urge to pick up the bottle, but he suppressed it and said in a barely audible whisper, "Fuck the woman with the children. Fuck her. I don't care about her or her bottle or anything. I don't have to care anymore, remember?"

Sadness and depression came rushing upon him, like a breath from the mouth of God. He felt his head grow heavy beneath it. The people on the bus were sad and tired and probably had no money. The woman had nothing to look forward to but endless years of wrestling with children. The smell of chemical deodorant coming from the bathroom in the back of the bus made everything seem cheap. And Foy was a sad little man talking to himself, obsessing over his thoughts, and for some reason fighting the urge to pick up a baby bottle.

Impulsively he jerked forward and started to reach for the bottle, but he stopped himself again and sank back into his seat. A wave of raw anger seized him. He clenched his teeth and stared at the tips of his shoes. He wanted to say something, and he wanted to say it out loud. He settled for a whisper that would be loud enough for people to hear but not understand.

"Oh yeah? How about this? Fuck everyone in the world but me! You like that?"

And then the anger left him as suddenly as it had come. He leaned forward until his forehead touched the back of the seat in front of him. His eyes filled with tears, and he rocked back and forth like an old Jewish man at the Wailing Wall. "I'm sorry. I'm sorry. I'm sorry. I didn't mean it."

Utterly broken, he got up from his seat, picked up the bottle, and handed it to the woman. She smiled at him and said, "Gracias, senior."

"De nada," he replied, surprised at himself for speaking Spanish. It was one of about four Spanish phrases he knew.

He flopped back into his seat and leaned his head on the window again, closing his eyes this time.

He whispered to himself without moving his lips. "De nada. De nada. Of nothing."

⁂

The bus made a squealing noise as it pulled into the New Orleans station. Foy, his face close to the window, surveyed his new surroundings.

Every place has its own look.

San Antonio looked dusty, with muted colors. Like it was the first hint of the West. New Orleans looked dark and rich, with deep colors. It was green and wet, and there were black people everywhere.

This is the beginning of the deep South. Everything east of here is like this.

Getting off the bus was a moment Foy had fantasized about for many years. Absolute freedom. No ties, no responsibilities, no one waiting for him, no one watching him to see how a minister would behave, no one to take care of, no schedule or agenda. He stood on the sidewalk outside the bus station. People hurried past him. They had places to go and things to do. Foy's destiny and direction were his own to choose. It was like a movie.

So how does it feel?

He stopped and his mouth opened a little. He lowered his chin and let it drift to the right as he tried to pay attention to what was going on inside him. He felt a nagging anxiety and a longing for a schedule and an agenda. This feeling disgusted him, but he tried to be gentle with himself.

It takes a while to get used to this. It's like going on vacation, but even harder. Just settle down; you'll be fine.

A college friend with some connections had gotten him a room above a retail space in the French Quarter. He had the address in his pocket but was self-conscious about hailing a cab, since he had never done that before. Plus he wanted to see and feel everything. That was part of the deal. Someone pointed down a street and said he could get to the French Quarter on foot. He slung his duffel bag over one shoulder and his backpack over the other and started walking.

A few streets down, a man was sitting on a piece of carpet, twisting and bending his body into extreme positions. There was a hat on the ground with some change in it. Most people walked by without even glancing at him. Foy was fascinated and watched him for a few minutes.

So you get up in the morning and walk out of your house carrying your carpet for a day of yoga or whatever and people give you money.

There wasn't much money in the hat. Foy dropped in some change and nodded to the man to show him that his odd skills were appreciated. The man saw his nod but gave no response, which amused Foy.

Nearby some boys were breakdancing on flattened, cardboard boxes. They had a hat on the ground too. A large pile of discarded batteries behind their boom-box indicated they had been at it for some time. It didn't seem that the money in the hat would cover the expense of the batteries, which bothered Foy. He looked around for an electric outlet and spotted one on the external wall of a nearby shop. He had a brief fantasy of bringing the boys an extension cord and being something of a hero, but when he played out the fantasy, it ended with the shopkeeper jerking the cord out of the wall and using it to drive the boys away. He decided they probably knew what they were doing and moved away.

In the French Quarter Foy was charmed to find that the streets were lined with two-story buildings that had wrought-iron balcony railings, just like in the photographs. He found his room and spent the afternoon doing things that people like to do in New Orleans. He had mile-high pie at The Pontchartrain and listened to jazz in a little club while drinking coffee with chicory in it. He went into a cigar store and asked for a really good cigar. He didn't know how to answer the shopkeeper's questions, so he just bought one that the man said was good. It was eleven dollars.

He found a café that looked right and sat outside smoking his cigar, drinking beer, and watching people walk up and down the street. It seemed strange to him, for some reason, that everyone had somewhere to go. The crowd flowed past the café like a river. People were in groups, laughing, drinking, and purposeful. He felt relaxed and at ease. He was not part of the scene. He was only watching.

So this is what you do. You go into the streets with your friends and walk up and down. You drink and talk and maybe you'll see something interesting. You do this a lot and eventually you're there when something interesting happens and you can tell the story at work or whatever. You have to be in this. This has to be your life. Natural. Just what you do.

The cigar started making him feel sick, so he stubbed it out and left it on the table with some money. Taking his beer, he moved out into the street to join the crowd. He paused at a strip club and peeked inside. The music was tacky and the woman on the stage looked tired. He grimaced and pulled his head out of the door quickly.

The crowd grew larger and moved down the street. Foy allowed himself to get caught up in it. A woman was throwing beads from a balcony and he caught a strand. The young men around him started yelling, "Show us your tits!" They said it over and over, and the woman looked like she was considering the proposition. He felt giddy for a moment and looked around.

I can do this if I want.

He joined the crowd and shouted, "Show us your tits!" but he was immediately uncomfortable and self-conscious. He only said it once. The woman quickly lifted her shirt, and Foy yelled along with everyone else and lifted his beer. But he hated the feel of it all, even before he lowered his arm. Nothing felt right. He was on the outside, looking in.

Shit, I don't even remember how to have fun. Maybe religion sucked the life right out of me, just the ability to hang out with some friends, get a little drunk, and enjoy whatever it is that they're enjoying. God, am I that lost?

Foy stopped in the middle of the street and became like an island, with people flowing around him. He began to push through the crowd, heading for the curb. As he moved he began to feel frantic. He had to get out of the street and over to the sidewalk where he could get his back against a building and watch things again. He wanted to feel the way he felt earlier, in the café.

When he reached the edge of the street, he noticed a battered Bible with no cover lying next to the curb in a pile of leaves. It lay open, as if someone was about to read it. The left side had a wet shoestring draped across it. A cigarette butt was wedged into the valley between the pages. A smear of mud obscured the page on the right.

It was such an ugly thing, like a corpse, and he could not control his reaction. He groaned and bent over it, as if it was a wounded puppy. He pulled the shoestring off and flicked the cigarette butt away. He turned a couple of pages back and forth.

It was a generic King James, the kind that are printed by the millions and spread all over the world like cheap toys and good-luck charms. The kind you find in motels, homeless shelters, and used book stores. The kind of Bible that people who never read the Bible own.

Foy stood up and looked down at the Bible, wiping his hands on his jeans. He felt a little resentful of its sudden appearance that evening.

This doesn't mean shit. Those cheap Bibles are everywhere.

He stood on the curb and looked back into the street. It was getting late and the crowd had grown even more, so that the street was almost full. The crowd's movement was fitful and sluggish. It stopped and started and surged here and there. Suddenly there was a commotion a short way down the street. There were angry voices and a burst of wild laughter. The movement of the crowd slowed and then stopped as people tried to see what was happening. By some miracle, the crowd parted unevenly and he could see all the way to the curb on the other side of the street.

Perfectly framed by the division of the crowd was a small, preteen girl sitting on the opposite curb. She was wearing jeans and a worn, faded T-shirt. Her tennis shoes were filthy and had no laces. In her hands was a flat box hanging from a rope that ran around her neck, like the cigarette-girl boxes from the old movies. Foy had never seen one of these boxes in real life, and he froze, staring at it. In the box were a few bags of potato chips and several varieties of candy. The girl was fidgeting, bouncing her right heel up and down at a furious pace.

Her shoulders were curved and slumped, and she had a vacant expression that looked as though it had settled into her face for good.

Foy realized, with a start, that this poor child was selling things in the middle of the French Quarter, all alone, late at night. He stepped off the curb into the street just as the crowd began to move again. The people flooded back together, blocking his view of the girl. He fought his way through the crowd but was dragged sideways by the current of people, so that when he arrived across the street he was about ten yards away from her. He turned his shoulders and walked hurriedly through the crowd, digging a hand into his pocket.

I'll buy everything she has in that box and just give her whatever cash I've got left. Maybe I should find out where she lives and take her home. She shouldn't be out here this late, working, selling stuff, whatever. That's gotta be against the law or something.

When he got to the place where he had seen the girl, she was gone. He looked around quickly, then sprang up on the base of a lamppost, like that guy in Singing in the Rain. He saw nothing but a river of bobbing heads. Across the street another young woman on a balcony pulled up her shirt. The crowd hooted and surged in that direction. Foy looked up at her. Her breasts were bouncing freely and she had a huge smile on her face. She looked so happy, like she was having the time of her life. Below her there was a chorus of cheers and dozens of hands raised beer bottles in a raucous toast.

Foy held onto the post with his right hand and swung around it, looking everywhere for the girl, but she was gone. Then, for some reason, he didn't like the idea of getting down, so he stayed on the lamppost, looking around in amazement.

I know nothing of this world. Nothing.

And then everything began to close in on him. The movement of the people below was repulsive, and he didn't want anyone to touch him. The sounds from the balcony were screeching and sharp, clawing at his mind. There was too much of everything, and he began to panic. He wanted to feel his back pressed against something large and solid. He wanted a safe place – his home or a room, just a small place with maybe one friend there to laugh with him. He wanted something familiar.

I don't want to be here. I don't like it here. I'm leaving and going to a place where I want to be.

He climbed down and started walking. Then the truth hit him hard. He had nowhere to go. He had no home and no family and no job. There was no one in the world for him. Not one person to know him and to know what he was feeling. He would not sit down with a friend tomorrow and say, "You can't believe what it was like out there on the street last night. There was this Bible and a little girl I saw." No one would hear this story.

Foy pressed his back against the front of a store. He was breathing hard, as if he had been running. A thought came to him that was cruel and mocking.

This is what it means to be lonely. And you are going to know what loneliness means.

if only

When a person dies, there is a sudden collapse of all that they knew. The complex and fragile framework of their worldview, which is a unique thing in all the universe, drops to the ground like the contents of a pricked water balloon. The depth of that loss is incomprehensible.

What is left after death are ghost-like shreds of your personality that live in the memories of those who knew you. Some warped version of you exists in the stories and the sorrow. And then those stories fade. The last to go are the memories of the one who loved you the most. Those memories are twisted and contorted into comforting shapes that he or she clings to for comfort. And then your beloved dies, and you are lost along with everything else that disappears in that terrible event.

After that is only what the children remember. It's not much when compared to the fullness of a life. And when those children die, there is only a name or maybe a faint memory on someone's family tree.

On a day and in a moment that no one knows, the last memory of you winks out of existence with the death of the last person who knew your name. And then it is as if you never lived. You join the ranks of the billions of humans who have walked this planet, living and loving and dying. Some were saints who lived and loved and died well. Others not so much. Some were scoundrels. All are forgotten.

It seems to me that the whole world would collapse if I were to die. How could things go on? How could the world continue without my worldview propping it up, explaining it, and giving it a purpose?

I look at the people around me—my friends and acquaintances. I cannot know them. They are walking mysteries. What they flash on their billboard faces and what words are released from their inner pravda are all that I can know. For a brief moment I want to know everyone. I want to see the world with everyone's eyes. For one, brief, god-wish moment. And then I settle back into reality. After all, I've come to love your billboard and your pravda. You take what you can get, right?

But there is one desire I have that cannot be sated. It cannot be satisfied, and it will not go away. It is a terrible loneliness to look into the eyes of the one you love and understand that you will never truly know her. You may know her better than anyone ever will, but you cannot know her. Her eyes are the windows of a strange, two-legged vessel that walks this earth for its allotted time. You stumble alongside her for years, but you may do nothing more than look into those eyes and hear again her best attempts to explain what goes on in her heart.

My wife's chocolate brown eyes look like they were transplanted from her father's face. She honors him by carrying those eyes for one more generation. The pure singleness of their color and the way she looks at you with no shame makes you know that you can trust her. You think she must be a gentle soul. These are things that anyone can know.

When I look into her eyes I bring something more to the experience. I know her life and her history and her ways. I remember her young heart, the one she had when we met at college. I remember her bouncing ponytail and purple pants. I remember her fears and joys as a young woman in seminary. I have seen her give birth three times and watched those children nurse at her breasts. I know her fierce integrity and her unwillingness to give up her innocence, which she holds just as fiercely. I know that she is what we call, "a good person." She wants goodness in the world. Truly wants it for herself and others. I know these things about her. I know more about Jeanene Atkinson than anyone else in the world ever will.

I have watched her age slowly over the years, softening, the skin around her eyes sagging a bit. The eyes themselves have not changed at all. Eyes are timeless in that way.

And now, God help me, she has a small pair of reading glasses that she shakes open sometimes and perches upon her nose. If I pull up a chair beside her I can watch her eyes darting back and forth, missing nothing in the fine print. Nothing but the truth will do for her, no matter how hard that truth may be. No skimming the words and wishing. Then she turns and her chin drops and her brown eyes look at me over the tops of those glasses. In that moment all the things I know about her press themselves together and try to force their way into my heart all at once. The cuteness of it. Adorable. Precious. Beyond words.

It hurts.

I want to stand at attention, draw my sword, and say, "I would die for you, my lady." I want to run circles around the couch with my arms out like airplane wings, shouting, "Look at me. I love you more than anyone ever did." I want to pull those eyes close, and make everyone go away. Go away! How dare you be here. How dare the earth and time hold anything but this moment. And I think this moment is owed to us, that the world should stop and there be nothing for as long as we need there to be nothing. And if time moves on and those eyes return to that paper, I feel that I've lost something which, in truth, I never had. And it's the saddest, loneliest thing to know it.

God, I wish I could get behind those eyes. Settle into the driver's seat and connect the wires to little electrode pads all over my body. I want to feel her woman heart. I want to know what it means to be her. What does this woman feel and think? More importantly, how does she feel and think? Could I take the knowledge all at once? Would I shiver, hold the sides of my head, and burst into tears? Does it take a long time to learn how to live with a woman's heart?

I can only imagine.

For now, there will be nothing but those eyes lifting above her glasses and the coy smile she has because she knows what those glasses do to me. For now, only her face with its thousands of movements that I parse and struggle to translate. For now, only language, which is such a crude instrument. Words are rusty, jagged, pig-iron tongs fumbling for purchase in the liquid silk of her soul.

For now, what love I have to give. Faith and hope will tear you apart with the rawness of their desire. But for now remains love, which is the greatest and only-est thing we have.

spam and grey poupon

Once I ate a piece of fried Spam with Grey Poupon on it. I was fully aware of the irony of this. Indeed, I took great pleasure contemplating it during the meal. And I thought it was delicious.

Whatever that says about me is true.

I like cake icing a lot. The more the better. The only thing that stops me from fighting children for the corner piece of cake at birthday parties is knowing I would look ridiculous. I will, however, try to position myself in line so that I might be given the corner piece. If handed the corner piece of cake, I will likely protest briefly, saying "that's way too much icing, but okay, if you insist."

Whatever that says about me is true.

I have loved Pepperidge Farm Goldfish Crackers for a quarter of a century. I only eat the Parmesan cheese version. Unfortunately, Pepperidge Farm has a problem with product consistency. Some Goldfish are salted less than others, and some are puffier with a powdery texture that I don't like. I learn the batch numbers and look through the packages on the shelves for good batches. Currently you should stay away from anything beginning with a D or a W. The RU series is pretty good.

Whatever that says about me is true.

I have always found it difficult to believe in things that seem unbelievable. When presented with a story in the Bible, I can't help running it through my epistemological filters. And if I don't think it happened, no amount of wishing, wanting, or denying can change my mind. I can gently avoid the subject. I can participate in the faith community's worship. I can appreciate the beauty of the scripture in question and even speak intelligently about its archetypal value in a world of human myth and dreams. But if I don't believe it, I just don't. I'm not proud of this. I'm not ashamed of it. It's simply a fact about me.

There is one exception to this. I have mustered enough emotional and mental energy to give assent to a small set of central Christian doctrines. This gift to God of my willing belief is the most sacred and vulnerable thing I can give to anyone.

It's the only thing I can give to the God who has everything. So I give it with love, knowing that it is a small and unimportant gift in the universe. I give this gift like a child who makes a homemade card and hopes his parents will put it on the front of the refrigerator.

Whatever that says about me is true.

I never got over not having a son, though I would not trade the three sisters for anything in the world, even a son. But that is a wound that will never heal. The only thing I have to give to the son I never had is carrying that sorrow and thinking about him sometimes. I still call him Elliot.

Whatever that says about me is true.

I can be a very crude and vulgar person, not out of malice or a desire to be rude or offend people. I just don't seem to have the same boundaries that other people have. Sex and death and bodies and fluids seem very natural to me. I think that words like shit or fuck or damn or hell are just words. A lot of very funny things involve crude or dark subjects, and coarse language is a part of human speech. If I'm with close friends, I can be pretty vulgar. But I try not to offend people who would be offended by that kind of thing.

Whatever that says about me is true.

I could go on and on. There are things about me that I'm ashamed of and will not speak of publicly. And there are things about me that are even goofier than these I have mentioned. There are silly parts of me, proud parts of me, and vain parts of me. Some parts of me you might find adorable. And there are some parts of me that, if you knew about them, you might say, "Dude, you have a problem."

To which I might say, "You mean a bigger problem than putting Grey Poupon on Spam, combing through bags of Goldfish Crackers in the supermarket, and bursting into tears when someone says Elliot?"

Now this is important. This is what I've been building to the whole time, though when I started this little piece weeks and weeks ago, I thought it would just be about putting Grey Poupon on Spam, which at the time seemed rather funny to me. But here we are at the end, and now something else has come to mind.

Whatever is true about you is true about you. I know that statement is absurd, but it works in the same way that "It is what it is" works. It's a good thing to say because we live in a culture that is heavily saturated with marketing, and it's easy for us to start thinking that what we say about ourselves is what's true.

It isn't.

What is true about you is what is true about you. And no amount of denying and pretending and covering up will ever change that. Sure, you can fool people for awhile, but you are the sum total of all the things that are true about you. And what we've always said about God is that God knows the truth about us.

Saying that God knows us is a spiritual statement of faith, but the deeper truth remains whether or not you believe in God. What is true about you is who you are. You are not who you want to be. You are not who you hope to be. You are not the person that others think you are.

You are the person who is defined by what you choose and what you truly desire and what you really think and believe. That's who you are. If you want to begin any kind of spiritual or metaphysical or personal journey, that's where you should begin. You should begin by owning who you are.

It's called spiritual poverty in our tradition. Jesus began his most famous words with this innocent sounding but profound statement:

"Blessed are the poor in spirit, for theirs is the Kingdom of Heaven."

If I was only allowed to keep one verse from the New Testament, that would be the one.

mouse turd on the communion table

Well, what would you have titled this?

Because there is really one one fitting title for this piece about the little present I found recently at the communion table. And turd is the only word that works in that title. Because turd is a great word. When you drop turd into a sentence, it shouts its presence with a coarse, rolling resonance that sounds like a springy sound effect in some cheap comedy.

Boi-oi-oi-oing.

My wife and I joined two friends recently in leading a retreat at a lovely retreat center on the Frio River in the Hill Country of Texas. The retreat ended, and we four presided over a communion table to celebrate our final time of worship with the group. I was setting up the communion elements while people were filing into the room for the service. That's when I noticed a mouse turd sitting right in the middle of the table.

At this point in the story, I'm afraid it's going to become quite clear that I'm not a normal sort of person. Your average person would have hurriedly disposed of the turd, following this with a thorough cleaning of the table. I, on the other hand, ran to get my camera. I began snapping shots of the turd. Close, far, with the macro function, without, turning the camera this way and that.

"Okay, mouse turd, work the camera. Yes. Beautiful. Give me some attitude. Sweet!"

"Why, why, why?" you ask me, shaking your head in disbelief. "Why would you take a picture of a mouse turd on a communion table?"

I actually didn't know at the time. I instinctively knew that this was a beautiful thing and a thing I would write about. I knew there was something important attracting me to this mouse turd. My policy in these situations is to take pictures first and ask questions later. And later I came up with the answer. I was attracted to the mouse turd because of its wonderfully earthy juxtaposition with communion, which is perhaps the holiest of moments in Christian worship. The whole thing reminded me of something I read about nativity scenes.

Ancient nativity scenes were not like the ones of today. Modern nativities usually contain nothing more than a stable with a few figures and animals gathered around the manger. Nativities from the 17th and 18th centuries in Spain and Europe often depicted the entire town of Bethlehem. The houses, the shopkeepers, the peasants, and the leaders of the town. The stable with the baby Jesus was only a small part of the whole.

And sometimes, squatting behind a door or hiding in some lonely corner of the nativity scene, you would find the Caganer.

The Caganer was a well-known figure. He wasn't as important as the Christ child or the Magi, but he was important enough to have an official name. The Caganer was a boy or a man with his pants down, taking care of business. Yes, going to the bathroom. Taking a dump. Why mince words? There was a statue of a man squatting behind the holy stable, sometimes with a fresh pile on the ground below him. Will euphemisms somehow make this more palatable for you?

"Why, why, why?" you ask me, shaking your head in disbelief. "Why would they put such a thing in the nativity scene?"

I'll tell you why. Because ancient people were not shy about earthy realities. Their religion was many things, but it wasn't afraid of the body or ashamed of it. That shameful stuff started with Queen Victoria, but that's another story for another day.

Spiritual leaders have long known that whenever we get too lofty, too spiritual, too separated from the body, God has other servants who bring us back down to earth. Children have a natural affinity for this kind of spiritual work. I was in a church service once when a little boy returned from the bathroom with his pants around his ankles and 6 feet of toilet paper sticking out of his bottom and trailing down the aisle like the devil's own bridal train.

Sometimes God's earthy servant is a person who simply will not be tamed. We once had a church member named Lyle, whose offenses against taste were so numerous and egregious that they cannot be listed here. For years I had to avoid making eye contact with Lyle during the sermon, lest he make some vulgar gesture that would cause me to laugh in the pulpit.

Lyle is not longer at our church, but I really miss him.

The forces behind these little church revolts are much like those behind real revolutions. When the government gets oppressive, the people revolt. If the revolution gets out of hand, a strong government rises to power. There's an inevitable, "Ying and Yang" to it all. You can count on it; when church people get too spiritual for their own damn good, one of God's other servants will bring us back to the body.

That's why I didn't flinch when I saw the mouse turd. I loved it. I've learned to watch for these earthy moments that pop up in the middle of all things holy and spiritual. They're funny, and they are a good sign that we might be taking ourselves a little too seriously.

On the night before communion, all through the house, God's children were sleeping, except for one mouse. After four days of prayers and singing and other religious hoo-ha, this little mouse—our own Caganer—crept into the room and mounted the communion table. He lifted his fur and left us a little present.

"There you go, humans. That's what I think of your religion, your cleanliness, your arrogance, and your pomp and circumstance. Here's an element you weren't expecting. Transubstantiate that, you bastards!

I do not know the mind of God. I have no idea what God contemplates or what amuses God. But if God's attention was drawn that night to our little mouse and his nefarious, after-hours activities, I bet God was smiling.

Heck, the whole thing might have been God's idea.

exegesis

So here's what you do. You take a phrase or a word or a short teaching out of the Bible. Something like "The book of life," or "The Son of Man," or "The Light of the World," or "No one comes to the Father but by me." These phrases could mean anything. They meant something in their day, surely, but the deepest and most scholarly study in the world cannot unravel exactly what they meant.

But you. You somehow know the truth. You take these phrases with no study at all, and you fill them with your theology, like someone filling helium balloons at a carnival. Then you hang a little basket below your balloons and float away, so delighted in the complex theological construct that you've put together. And from your elevated position you lay burdens on people that you could never keep yourself. Lightning bolts thrown down from the sky. Zeus never wielded as much power.

You are going to hell for your lack of faith or for your participation in a religious life or non-religious life that I don't understand and therefore don't approve of.

You may not be a sexual person, but you must live in strict, celibate loneliness. You will fall in love many times over the years, but you must deny your love and break your own heart over and over and over again, all the days of your life. (And this from a preacher who can't say no to a second bowl of ice cream.)

You must believe the things I tell you about the world, the earth, the sky, the stars, and God. You must give intellectual consent to all parts of my message. And if you cannot believe what I say, SHAME on you! Shame on you even if you tried very hard to believe but could not.

Give me your life; give me your money; give me your mind; give me your time. Give me all of these things, and I shall take them from you and use them to fill up more balloons so that I can fly higher and throw my lightning bolts down on more people.

And the hard thing for me is that you think this is the right way to treat the Bible and the mysterious phrases found within it. In your mind, you are the great Bible scholar, while I am a little weak in this regard. Weak and liberal and not very serious about the Bible.

For I, in my weakness, can hardly stand before the mystery of the ancient scriptures. I am hurt by them, filled with joy by them, angered by them, and sometimes inspired by them. And often I can do nothing more than confess my own confusion and brokenness.

You shake your head at me and say, "What kind of a minister are you? Don't you believe the Bible?"

And I look back at you, just as puzzled. "Believe the Bible?" What does that even mean? I say it over and over to myself.

"Believe the Bible. Believe the Bible. Believe the Bible. Believe the Bible."

Eventually the word "believe" starts to sound like something you do with your hands. Like punching something or pushing a vacuum cleaner around. Like you could believe the Bible all over the house and then out into the front yard, where you could believe it around in little circles while waving to the neighbors. Then you could believe the Bible back into your house and store it in the closet, where you keep it until you feel like believing it out in public again.

Do I believe the Bible? I'm trying to know the Bible. And by knowing, I mean the way that Adam knew Eve, and the way that the Creator knows us. I mean the kind of knowing that is like falling in love. I'm trying to love/know the Bible. And I will always struggle with how I can love/know the scriptures when some parts are so hard and mean and awful that you feel bad for even reading them. And then some parts are so beautiful that you can't stop crying when they whisper little hints of truth and mystery to you.

So that's all I've got. Whatever that says about me is what I am. I'm less sophisticated and more unsure than when I began years ago as a young minister. I'm tired and fairly broken myself. I just turned 47, so I'm half dead if I live to be an old man, and more than half dead if I don't. So there's just no time left, really. No time for talking or fighting or judging.

It seems like it is the time for listening and loving and accepting all who seek truth in peace and are open-minded enough to confess that they are simply not up to the task.

thoughts on depression after two years of medication

It's been just about a year since I wrote about my ongoing struggle with depression.

So, how are things, you ask.

Just fine. Good. Mostly good. I think good. I've been on Wellbutrin for over a year now. Three little white pills every morning. I don't ask questions; I just take them.

I think this is the way I'm supposed to feel. I remember feeling like this before. I get happy and excited about things now. I get sad sometimes, but the sadness seems appropriate. It comes and it goes. I'm an introspective kind of guy, so a certain amount of ennui is in my makeup.

So, good, I think. I'm feeling good.

But I have lost something over the last two years. What depression took from me was my simple way of thinking about the human psyche. Depression has made things messy for me, and it has made me much more forgiving and gentle when I meet people who are emotionally out of control.

I used to think that the human mind divided neatly into two spheres, a right and a left. It's a metaphoric division, of course, but yeah, two sides that one imagines could be pulled apart like two halves of an orange. Left brain and right brain. Your basic dualism. That sort of thing.

We think and we feel. We have reason and we have emotion. Of the two kinds of human experience, the emotional part was not to be trusted, as far as I was concerned. Not in relationships; not in daily living; and most of all, not in the spiritual realm. I have always had a deep fear and loathing of overly emotional religion.

Emotion, it seemed to me, was very arbitrary. It often led you in the wrong directions. It made you do things that did not make sense. Whereas the rational part of the human mind was careful and reasoning and able to see truth, even through a fog of emotion.

I proudly labeled myself as a cerebral person. I spent a lot of time thinking and talking and arguing and reasoning. Not so much time feeling things. I thought I was in control of all that silly, emotional stuff. I felt numb, mostly. And I assumed that you weren't feeling things unless you, well, FELT them.

Oh, you feel things. Here's a shocker. No one feels things in more dangerous ways than the person who thinks he feels nothing. That's the guy you have to watch out for.

Jung said it this way: If you do not come to terms with your shadow side, the opposite of your strengths, you will be ruled by that shadow side. I believe that now. In my case, all of my unexplored feelings were sucked into a vortex of anger. Of course, I was too sophisticated to let my anger out in healthy ways. So I ate my anger. I ate it dry. It was like swallowing unshelled peanuts. It did not sit well in my gut.

That's when depression exploded my simple ways of thinking. You can say whatever you want about the emotional side of human beings, but emotions rule the day. They dictate our actions FAR more than we think. People live right out of their guts. We are primitive in that way.

When my depression became critical, it rose from beneath me like a dark wave. It tossed me about, laughing at my feeble words of protest. It kicked my ass, but good. I was unable to act in ways that made sense. My feelings of sorrow and panic washed away my control like a tsunami washes away the hammocks hanging near the beach.

I hid my sorrow as long as I could, and then I began to pick compulsively at the skin on my right hand until it bled. It hurt so bad and I would swear I would never do it again. But then my left hand would start creeping over to my right hand. I couldn't stop it.

So much for Mr. Cerebral.

And then, just to make sure that my worldview was completely shattered, that one stone was not left standing on another, and that salt was sown in my fields, I began to think crazy thoughts. Depression made me think crazy things.

THINK them.

I

Thought

Crazy

Things

I had thoughts that were not based in reality. Do you know how frightening and horrifying that is to a person like me?

At one point I decided that my wife of twenty years no longer loved me. I thought that, baby. THOUGHT IT.

And I thought that the people in my church didn't like me anymore and were probably talking about how to fire me without totally devastating our family. I figured they would be nice in the way they did it, but yes, people were talking about me and trying to find a way to get rid of me.

Um, that's some crazy shit. I am many things, but unloved and unappreciated are not among them.

So I was wrong about all of it. The simple division between thought and emotion, the control I thought I had by denying things I felt, and my arrogant pride in thinking that I understood myself well enough to have clear thoughts.

That's what depression took from me.

What's left? Let's see…

A lot of humility and grace. I feel sorrow when I see men whose faces are hard and whose anger is beyond their control. I wish I could make them little boys again and hold them in my lap.

A new respect for people who deal well with their emotions, trusting them and experiencing them and nurturing them.

Gratitude for how I feel. Feeling good is very nice. I like it. I like to see my daughters and feel happy about it. I like to look forward to doing things instead of just doing them because duty calls.

Silliness. I'm such a silly person. You can't believe how silly I am. I'm the silliest person in our whole family. Just a silly, giddy, goofy, funny boy.

Spiritual joy. I feel a deep, wondrous joy about my spiritual journey. Paying ritual homage to the power/intelligence behind the cosmos is a rich and meaningful thing to me. It is closely tied to humility. In the absence of any hope of figuring things out all by myself, I join myself to pilgrims across the ages, singing songs, reciting poetry, and telling sacred stories under the stars. Depression stole the joy from my faith, and I'm glad to have it back.

And last, love. Love was left behind after the depression went away. I've rediscovered love, and it's like finding a baby bunny hiding under a zucchini leaf. You may pick her up and hold her, but be very careful. She's trembling. But isn't she the sweetest thing you've ever seen?

I think that this will be my last depression entry. I've said enough, and now is the time for living. If something happens and I get in bad shape again, I'll be honest and tell you about it. Until then, if you don't hear from me, assume that no news is good news.

the coin and the question

A Real Live Preacher Dramatized Version.

Saul was dressed in an expensive, imported robe. He was obviously a wealthy man. His hair gleamed and was heavy with Persian oil. His beard was trimmed short in a manner that was trendy among local Romans. He wore expensive jewelry, including a number of rings. One of them bore the mark of King Herod Antipas, for Saul was an official in his court. He stood with several other Herodians outside of Antipas' palace in Jerusalem.

A group of Pharisees wearing simply adorned but elegant robes came down the street. They were huddled closely together and avoided contact with anyone walking near them. Their heads were wrapped with leather bands holding phylactery boxes on their foreheads. Their beards were long and flowing, as were the tassels dangling from the corners of their robes. They slowed as they approached Saul and the men with him. The two groups looked at each other warily.

Saul stepped forward and held out his forearm to one of the Pharisees, inviting a Roman handshake. He was refused, as expected. He winked at his friends.

"Hello, Mathias."

One of the Pharisees, apparently the leader, nodded.

Saul continued. "We don't see you in this part of town often. I hope you didn't brush against any loose women on your way here or dirty your clean robes on our common streets."

The men behind him laughed, and the faces of the Pharisees tightened. Mathias spoke sharply in response.

"Always making jokes, Saul. Just like when we were boys, and you laughed after being thrown out of the synagogue for acts of wanton profanity. Still whoring for the Romans, are you? Still have your nose up the ass of that jackal Herod, may God smite him and all such lawbreakers and traitors."

Several of the Herodians put their hands on their swords and stepped forward. The Pharisees neither laughed nor made any defensive move. They stood motionless. Saul held up his hand. He spoke a few sentences in Latin to the men behind him, and they relaxed. He turned back to Mathias with a smile on his face.

"Let us put this aside for now and deal with the problem at hand. We have considered the matter, and I think we have the perfect solution."

He reached into a belt and pulled out a coin. He flipped it toward Mathias, who caught it, looked at it in his palm, and then dropped it as if it had burned him. The Pharisees looked at the silver denarius laying in the dust and took a step away from it. Mathias looked enraged, but he swallowed hard and forced a calm expression on his face.

"I'll have to go home and wash now before I enter the Temple. Thank you so much, Saul. Is it not enough that you abandon the faith of our fathers? Do you also have to ridicule and pollute those of us who remain true to God?"

Saul stepped forward and retrieved the coin. He tossed it in the air and caught it again.

"All that fuss over a coin with the head of Caesar on it. It is not an idol. It is legal tender. Your religious ways are hopelessly outdated and irrelevant in the modern world. Still, it is precisely this reaction that will allow us to trap him. We'll all go together to the temple tomorrow. Jesus will undoubtedly be speaking to his rabble near there. You can simply ask him if it is permissible under the law of Moses to pay taxes to Caesar or not. If he says yes, you can blather on about how he's gone soft on the Roman question, or how he breaks the commandments without a second thought. Whatever you want to say. You can spin it however you like."

"And if he says that it is not lawful to handle this money at all, much less pay taxes with it?"

Saul grinned. Malice glittered in his eyes.

"Then I will have him scourged and in the court before Herod within the hour. And that will be the last that anyone will hear from Jesus of Nazareth."

꒰ꆤ ꒰ꆤ ꒰ꆤ ꒰ꆤ ꒰ꆤ

Jesus sat on an elevated platform near the court of the Gentiles, surrounded by a crowd of about 75 people. There were both tradesmen and laborers present along with women and a number of children. Some of the children were listening to Jesus. Others were sitting on the ground drawing in the dirt with sticks. Jesus was in the middle of one of his famous stories, and the crowd was completely engrossed in the tale. Near the back of the crowd were a couple of temple guards who had wandered over to listen.

As Jesus spoke, his eyes lifted and he looked over the heads of the crowd at something behind them. He continued to talk, but his eyes did not return to the people, and he seemed somewhat distracted. Jesus slowed his story and then stopped speaking altogether. Some people turned around to see what he was looking at. Jesus stroked his beard thoughtfully.

"My my, look who's coming down the street toward us."

The rest of the crowd turned in time to see ten men approaching, five Pharisees and five Herodians. The people respectfully parted and allowed the men up close to Jesus.

"Pharisees and Herodians on the streets together?" Jesus held up his hands in disbelief and addressed the crowd.

"Why it must be the long-awaited year of Jubilee. Peter, I thought you were keeping an eye on the calendar for us. Jubilee has come, and I've been paying rent on my father's land for half the year!"

Peter grinned, and the crowd laughed loudly. Jesus laughed too, bending at the waist and nodding to the people around him.

"Good one, right? Of course good."

The ten men said nothing. They waited patiently for the laughing to stop. As the sounds died out, Jesus straightened and spoke.

"Good afternoon, Mathias. You certainly have some surprising new friends with you."

There were a few chuckles, but the crowd sensed that something important was happening and quieted quickly.

Mathias nodded to one of the other Pharisees, who stepped forward to address Jesus.

"Rabbi, a question, please."

Jesus stepped down from the platform and went to the man. He touched him on the arm and nodded.

"Certainly. What would you like to know?"

The man looked a little uncomfortable to have Jesus suddenly so close to him. He cleared his throat and offered an obviously prepared speech.

"Good rabbi, it is well known that you are among the wisest rabbis, not only in Nazareth, but yes, even here in Jerusalem. Your wisdom is known far and wide."

Jesus inclined his head politely.

"Further, we know that you are dedicated to God's truth. You do not worry about your reputation or the reputation of others. You simply tell the truth and never let any human concerns deter you. You are to be congratulated for this. And this is why we seek your counsel. We want to know the truth about a difficult matter."

Jesus inclined his head again.

"Is it correct under the law of Moses to pay taxes to Caesar, or not?"

Jesus did not hurry. The ball was in his court and he intended to keep it there for awhile. He nodded and considered the issue. An exaggerated frown came onto his face and he looked at Mathias. Jesus nodded to him, as if he was offering congratulations. He then moved his gaze over to the Herodians. He looked into Saul's eyes seriously. Saul looked amused and held his gaze. Jesus slowly looked at Saul's hair and clothing. He looked down Saul's robes to his expensive sandals and then back up again. Then he turned to the man who had asked the question.

"Yes, an excellent question. A very good question. Particularly since we are in the presence of some who are so dedicated to the love of God and the keeping of the Law. And others who are..." He glanced at the Herodians "...equally passionate about the laws of Rome."

Jesus lifted his chin so that it was obvious he was addressing the crowd.

"And I shall give them an answer. Yes, I shall. But first, does anyone happen to have one of those coins we use to pay our taxes to Rome? The silver denarius. You know the one."

The crowd whispered. Some muttered and others allowed their faces to show their disgust.

One of the Herodians stepped forward and held a coin out to Jesus.

"Thank you, good sir. We are fortunate that the Pharisees and their Herodian friends have brought one of the coins in question with them. And he had it so readily available. Right there in his pocket; just like that."

Many in the crowd laughed and whispered to each other. The Pharisees looked uncomfortable and embarrassed. A couple of them inched farther away from the Herodians.

Jesus reached for the coin but then pulled his hand back suddenly. He fumbled in his robe until he found a small cloth. He waved it to the crowd, and then took the coin from the man with the cloth, being very careful not to let it touch his hands.

"I don't carry these coins myself, of course. Don't even like to touch them, what with the second commandment and all. So I'm glad these gentlemen had one handy."

The crowd burst into laughter. The Pharisees' faces darkened with anger, and they shifted their weight back and forth uncomfortably.

Jesus turned and mounted the raised platform again.

"I wanted to look at the coin so we could see whose face is on it. Whose face is this anyway?"

Jesus acted as though he had never seen a silver denarius before. One of the Herodians said, "Caesar's."

Jesus looked surprised. "Oh, Caesar." He looked at the head on the coin lying on the cloth in his hand. Then he prodded the underside of the cloth with a finger, flipping the coin over, seeing now the image of a woman seated on a throne. "And this must be his lovely mother Livia on the other side." He turned his head slightly and made a mock spitting sound, "Ptuh, ptuh, ptuh." The crowd roared again. One older man laughed so hard he began to choke. A friend pounded him on the back, causing another wave of laughter to rise from the crowd.

Jesus motioned with his free hand to quiet everyone, as if the crowd was being rude and he was trying to get them to be a little more polite.

"Now, now, please."

When the crowd was silent, Jesus looked directly toward the ten men.

"Well then, why don't you return to Caesar what belongs to Caesar, and give to God what belongs to God."

He tossed the coin back toward the ten men, letting the cloth flutter to the ground. As the coin flew toward the center of the group, the Pharisees backed away. But one of the Herodians caught the coin and held it defiantly in his fist. Jesus fell silent and stood staring at the men. The people in the crowd stared at them as well. The men waited to see if Jesus had anything else to say. He did not.

There was no easy way to leave. That became apparent, so the men turned a few at a time, trying to look dignified, and walked away. As the last of them was leaving, Jesus called out.

"Mathias!"

Mathias stopped and turned around.

"I know you, and I know your family. You're better than this. And you're not the sort of man who would normally cast his lot with the Herodians. There are some things more polluting even than the Romans and their money. Think on these things."

Mathias stared back at Jesus. He licked his lips once, started to say something, then turned and walked away.

Information for those not familiar with the gospels or the culture of that day:

This story is found in all three synoptic gospels (see Matthew 22:15–22, Mark 12:13–17, Luke 20:20–26). My dramatization draws upon all three. There are only subtle differences between the versions.

The Pharisees were religious conservatives, we might say, while the Herodians were supporters of the very secular King Herod, who was a Jew, but in name only.

Some scholars think that the Jewish people of that time were in a bind when it came to Roman taxes. Rome required that they pay taxes, among them a poll tax. Rome issued a special silver denarius for that particular tax. This coin had the head of Caesar on one side and a picture of his mother on the other. An inscription around the head said that Caesar was divine, making this an idol and a clear violation of the Second Commandment, which prohibits making graven images of God. Everyone probably paid the tax, but there was a lot of theoretical discussion about whether or not doing so put one in violation of the religious laws.

The Jewish Jubilee year was supposed to come at the end of every 49 years. Every seventh day was a sabbath day, every seventh year a sabbath year, and every 49 years a Jubilee. The Jubilee year was to be marked by some fairly radical moves toward justice and reconciliation, including this unusual practice: All lands returned to their original owners. This kept all the wealth and power from accumulating in the hands of a few. So even if a poor family lost their land and had to pay rent to use it, in the Jubilee year they would get their land back. I have read that it is unclear whether the Jubilee year was ever actually practiced. The economic chaos that would have resulted from carrying out the command might have been thought to pose too great a threat to order. Even if it was not practiced, the Jubilee year would still have been a symbol of future justice.

The joke I have Jesus telling is not in the original accounts. But it allows me to emphasize how strange it would have been for Pharisees and Herodians to be together.

And original hearers of this story would likely have known that. It would almost have to be the Jubilee year for Pharisees and Herodians to be working together.

slow church

When Philip Gröning wanted to make the documentary "Into Great Silence," he asked the Carthusian monks at the Grande Chartreuse monastery in France if he might spend a couple of years quietly filming their lives. They said they would think about it and get back to him. Sixteen years later he received a letter from them. They had considered his request and were now ready for him to begin filming.

What kind of slow-moving world do these monks inhabit? Sixteen years in the modern world is time enough for two or even three careers. Why would these monks assume Philip Gröning was still interested in this project or even interested in filming anything at all? How did they find his address after sixteen years? Did someone write it on a scrap of paper and keep it in a box all that time?

The monks of Grande Chartreuse mark time in their own way. Time in their world moves more slowly. Things unfold gradually. Nothing happens quickly, so when things do happen they are important things. Things that seemed important or even urgent one year might not be so important a year later. After sixteen years, people may have forgotten them altogether. Consider for a moment how important a thing must be if it passes the deep consideration and patient process of the Carthusians of Grande Chartreuse.

While our church does not move as slowly as these ancient monks, we are a very slow church. When I am at our church I can hear the people of our world rushing by on the highway while I mark steps down the path to the labyrinth. A car that passes our church might travel a mile before I take another step. Five miles while I consider a painted rock left on the ground by a child. Which of us do you think is actually getting somewhere?

Near the front of our main building sit two rather mysterious slabs of concrete with pink and green paint on the top. They are benches dropped off some five years ago by a woman who thought they might make a nice addition to the church. We talked about it at our next elders' meeting. Not everyone was convinced we needed benches, though we all allowed they might be nice. One person wasn't crazy about the colored paint. Others didn't mind it. The general consensus was that someone should probably figure out how to put the benches together and do it. A year or so later, it was brought up again. There wasn't much energy for the project, but again we agreed that someone should probably go ahead and put those benches together. Another year went by. The concrete blocks sank softly into the earth, the way things do when they sit in one place for long time. New people at our church sometimes wonder what they are. One man told me he assumed they were monuments of some kind. The pink and green paint, still visible, has outlasted anyone who might question how well it fits into the color palette of the land. The benches have become the land, so their color IS the color of the land.

And now these stacks of concrete are indeed a monument. Little children sit on them, for they are the right size, having never been assembled. Boys leap off them, kicking their feet in the air, lost in some imaginary game. I love them as they are and would be heart-broken were I to arrive one day and find that they had actually been put together after all these years.

People tell me that the average stay for a pastor in an American church is eighteen months. That astounds me. We might have a stack of rocks on our back porch for eighteen months while we talk about what we should do with them. Most of our best stories span five or six years at least. It takes about a decade just to figure out what's going on at our church.

So we are a slow church. It is our nature. Many of us are tired of churches that have freshly printed agendas at every meeting and high energy, executive types barking orders and getting things done. We tend to attract wounded, introverted sorts who need to sit in the woods for a while. Maybe for two or three years. The average time it takes to get a project completed at Covenant Baptist Church is three years. Someone brings up an idea. It gets talked about for a few months, maybe put on the elders' agenda. If it is still being talked about a year later, we might talk seriously about it. Often someone joins the church who has a passion for this project and gets it going in earnest, like when then Soupiset family joined and got the labyrinth project moving after years of discussion and dreaming.

Unfortunately, the pace of our church frustrates some people. People who have a strong need to make lists and get things done in short order go crazy here. People who don't like nonsense are uncomfortable here because much of what we do is nonsense, in that we often have no sense of where we are heading

Turtles All The Way Down

with what we are doing or what it will be whenever we finish it. But God bless the delightful souls who cannot abide this place. We don't worry about them. You can find high-achieving churches on almost every street corner these days. And God bless those churches too, because there are a lot of things that need to be done in our world. But there also should be slow churches, churches where you can stop and catch your breath. We've decided that our calling is to be one of those. We are a church for people who feel their life speeding along like those moving sidewalks in airports, and they want to get off for a time. We're strolling through life here, meandering along at our own spiritual pace.

If you are thinking we don't get anything done, nothing could be further from the truth. We do things. We just do them slowly. With time as no burden or constraint, we find we can do a lot with our bare hands. Children built our rock-lined path through the woods. Children working with their hands the last Sunday morning of each month. It took two years, but why should that matter? I watched a lot of the construction process. The man who guided them was in no hurry and didn't mind if they lengthened the path only a few feet a month. The children were laughing. They had fun. And they built something our community loves.

There are lighted paths here and quiet, unassuming buildings, beautiful in their timidity. We built these paths and buildings. It just took us a long time. There are strange plants in their native habitat, some of them thorny and dangerous. We move slowly when we build things, so the plants are not disturbed. There are cactus blooms and wildflowers and even native chili peppers that grow wild. You can eat them if you know where to find them. There is a rock in the building with a man's name on it. There is a pile of wood that has never been used but has a great story behind it. There is a giant tree with a strand of weathered beads near it. We cleared a circle around this tree and made it a sacred place. It only took us five years to do that.

So you see, things get done here. But they are slow things. They are things with natural patinas that can only grow with time. Things are settled into the ground and beautiful. These things exist because we've chosen to live our lives slowly and deliberately in this community.

We're living on Spirit time, not clock time.

This piece was originally published at the High Calling Blog Network. Http://HighCallingBlogs.com

olives, wineskins, white bread, and jesus

I ate a whole can of olives the other day. Is that bad? It doesn't seem bad. Olives are fruit, right? I've never heard anyone refer to olives as fruit, but they're plants and plants are generally good for you. They are very salty, which I think might not be good. Salt is one of those things they used to say was good for you and they even handed out salt tablets to athletes. Then I think they said it was bad for you and everyone was trying to cut down on salt. But I don't hear so much about salt anymore. I think maybe it's bad but not as bad as, say, eating nothing but fast-food all the time. Compared to that, eating a can of olives might even be kind of good for you.

One would think so, anyway.

I can't keep up with this stuff, to tell you the truth. When I eat I have to look over at my wife and say, "Is this bad for me?" She seems to know about these things. Take bread, for example. Years ago, bread was fattening and something you had to watch out for. But then everyone said it was red meat you had to avoid. Red meat would clog up your arteries. So bread wasn't that bad. But then suddenly they said meat was okay as long as you avoided bread completely. And there were those diets where you ate no bread at all or anything even remotely resembling bread.

So bread has been sometimes good and sometimes bad for us. I don't mean white bread, of course. I think white bread became bad for us sometime back in the 70s and has remained bad ever since. I think it has stayed bad the whole time. That's okay, Jeanene got me used to wheat bread years ago, and now white bread gives me the creeps. The way you can roll it into little balls and it turns kind of gray if your hands weren't all that clean. I never liked that about white bread, even when I was a kid, even before it was bad for us.

Anyway, it seems to me that a guy ought to be able to eat a can of olives and it not be all that bad for him. Not with all the white bread and fast food and sweatshops overseas and the horrible stuff they're putting all over the Internet.

But none of this really matters because when I ate that can of olives, it wasn't nearly as good as I thought it was going to be. I probably won't do that again anyway. When it comes to food, I should probably just move my fork slowly toward things and watch Jeanene for cues. She could give me a nod or a wince or a strong, stern shaking of the head. Then I would know what things are currently bad for me because, like I said, somehow she seems to know about this stuff.

I'll tell you another thing I can't keep straight is the Church. And I went to seminary and even graduated from it. I don't know how you non-seminary folks are keeping up with what's good and bad in church.

When I was a kid, taking care of your Bible was a good thing. You got a Bible for a present or something and you wrote your name in it. And you never put things on top of it because that didn't show respect. And you kept that Bible for a long time because that was YOUR Bible. You kept it for years and it would get all worn and everything, which you were sort of proud of because it showed you were reading it.

But then there were new translations coming out every month or so, and Bibles got cheap to buy. You can even get them in grocery stores now. And some people said that if you were too devoted to one copy of the Bible it was its own kind of weird idolatry. So now people can pretty much do whatever they want to their Bibles. Toss them around. Lose them and just buy a new Bible. Whatever.

And I remember when all we sang in church were hymns, except at church camp where you could sing all these other cool songs with guitars around the campfire. And then some people started singing some of the campfire songs right in church, which seemed okay. But then others said it wasn't good because those camp songs supposedly aren't as theologically sound as the old hymns. But then the people who liked the camp songs said that they are mostly made of words right out of the Bible, so you can't exactly say they shouldn't be sung in church. And then the hymn people grumbled, and the campfire people grumbled, and this is the truth: I don't know what we should or shouldn't be singing in church, if anything.

To be honest, I don't think anyone knows quite what to do in church anymore. For years church people told us that homosexuality was evil and not just a sin but a very bad sin. They had us all scared of homosexuals, that we might even become one or something if we were around them. And you just assumed that the Bible was chock-full of commandments about homosexuals and them even going to hell for being that way. I mean, you just assumed that because the church people were so sure of themselves and talked about it like it was a fact.

But then some people started reading the Bible very carefully, all the parts people said were about homosexuality. And some of them said, "Oh shit! The Bible hardly says anything about homosexuality at all. And what it does say is pretty hard to understand." So those people said we should just leave homosexuals alone and let them come to church and let their relationships be between them and God, like all relationships are.

But now, see, the ones who thought homosexuality was a really bad thing were getting tired of the changes. It seemed like you hardly heard a hymn in church anymore, and people were dressing sloppy on Sundays, and women were preaching, and you could hardly find a King James Bible anywhere. So I think they just decided to dig their heels in on this whole homosexuality thing. And it became like a religious war. It's gotten so bad that even the Episcopalians are fighting over it. And that's scary because you expect the Baptists will make fools of themselves over stuff like this, but we've always counted on the Episcopalians to keep their wits about them. We count on the Episcopalians to be careful and not to allow themselves to get so divided over something that they might actually split their church in two.

I mean, the Episcopalians can be kind of stuffy and all, and who knows what the hell they're doing with all the chants and walking up and down the aisles before church, and what with the banners and all the different colors all the time. But my goodness, they're the smartest ones of all of us church kind of people. If they can't figure this homosexual thing out, what hope is there for the rest of us?

And all the while people who aren't in the Church are just standing there watching it all, and they have no idea what all the fuss is about and neither do a lot of us who've been in the Church all of our lives. We don't know either. Maybe in a few years the Church will be all busted up and the only thing left will be people gathering in small groups here and there, and it might not be anything like it is now.

That's what Jesus was saying with that stuff about the wineskins. How the truth about God cannot be held in old wineskins because they will just burst. And sometimes that's what happens with the Church. It bursts like a dried-out wineskin and you have to find a new wineskin.

And it's always hard for the church people who live in a time when the wineskins are bursting. It's hard on that generation, but there's nothing you can do about it. Nothing at all but just wait and try to be as true as you can and keep your eyes open for what comes next.

a one-size-fits-all parable

I can't believe it.

You wanted to know the truth.

Yeah, but...

That's why I warned you. But you had to know.

I still can't believe it.

"I want to know the truth. About God, Jesus, who shot JFK, life, Darwin, all of it." That's what you said; that's what you told me.

But I just. I don't want to know this. I don't know what to do now. How to act or how to be.

You'll find a way to deal with it. Everyone does. It's all part of the journey.

So that guy was right?

What guy?

That one guy. Who was always saying that stuff about, you know, all that stuff we talked about. I hate that guy. He was right?

Yep.

See, that's the part that really gets me. I mean it's all shocking, but that guy was right? THAT GUY?

Well, technically he was wrong too, but he was more right than you were. Technically. Of course, it depends on how you look at it.

What do you mean?

Well, if he was here—if your positions were reversed—I'd be telling him that you were right. Or more right than he was anyway.

What? You mean everyone's right?

I wouldn't say that. No.

Everyone's wrong?

More or less. If you feel like you have to say something, I guess that's the best way to say it. Yeah, everyone's wrong.

Oh my God. Wait. Should I say that now? Now that...

No one cares if you say that or don't.

Okay. Oh my God. My life. What was I living for? What were we all living for? Think about how much time I ... all the arguments, the hours I spent talking like I knew something, thinking I really did know something.

Stop.

What? What did I do?

Nothing. Just stop. Right now, how you feel—bewildered, lost, unsure, humble, insignificant.

Yeah.

That's how you're supposed to feel. You really are a very small creature in this universe. And now you know that. I guess you always knew it, but now you REALLY know it. So however you got here, it's okay because you're here and you're the way you're supposed to be.

Oh, so that's why everyone is...

Wrong?

Yeah.

Right.

Heh. That's really funny, now that I think about it.

Ooh, you've added a little humor to the mix. Very nice. Yes, you're ready. Don't say anything else. No, don't speak. Don't think anything else. Just stay like you are right now.

You're ready to begin.

a love letter for redeemed pagans and lost christians

There is only one righteous way for you to be saved if you've spent too much time in the Church. You must lay your religion down. Lay it down hard. Drop it. Leave it on the trail and walk away from it. And you have to mean it. You can't fake this. You have to renounce religion and leave it for good. As far as you know, you'll never pick it up again.

After that you can walk freely in the wild places where faith can still be found. As you walk, stretch out your arms and touch the foliage on either side of the trail, because these trees are the borders of your faith and this earth your true home. And every leaf jutting into your path is itself a fossil, laid down before the ages, suddenly exposed and within hand's reach along the cut edges of the trail.

Who laid bare these leafy walls? Who cut this covenant trail and left these leaves exposed to my eyes and my hands and my mind?

If fear has seized your heart, and you want to look back at what you left behind, hear this: There are no religions of The Word. Because if there is a Word, our frail ears can't hear it. What we have are religions that clamor after The Word and talk about The Word and market The Word and brand themselves as keepers of The Word. It's all best guesses and hearsay, and if you can't own up to that and still keep faith with your brothers and sisters, you're just fooling yourself and maybe that's okay with you. That's all some people want – to be nicely and gently and comfortably fooled.

I know the Bible, for I have spent half a lifetime looking there, but it cannot give you The Word. And if you treat those words as if they were The Word, then the Bible will be dead to you. The stories will turn their faces away from you, fold their robes over their shoulders and go to sleep.

So you won't have the Bible to cling to. I'm sorry.

But there is earth for your feet and air for your lungs and stars for your eyes and flesh for your desire. All religion begins with these, and if you ever lose them you have lost your roots and your guts. You'll have your precious scriptures, but they will be like desiccated skin stretched over bleached bones. No flesh or desire there.

Start with what you can see and feel and touch. Start with what makes you cry. And if you do not cry, ask yourself why not. Start with what brings you joy. And if you feel no joy, ask yourself why not. Start with what draws your eye and your attention and your obsessions. And if you do not see or notice or obsess, ask yourself why not.

Start with these things and pay attention to your dreams and to myths, which are the common dreams of all humanity. Come as a child, naked and innocent, and the myths will jump to life. The stories will awake, uncover their faces and hold you gently with such a lovely and old embrace that you will cry. You will feel joy. You will see and by seized by the truth.

Now STOP! Stop right there. Repent. Turn around and go back down the trail to retrieve the religion you left behind. You were fearful to leave it, but returning to it now is terrifying; I know. Take up your religion, for now it has no power to curse you but only the power to bless. Take it up like a man takes up his grandfather's worn tools. Take it up like a child cupping a palm of water from a spring. Take it up like a woman lifting her man's hand to her lips.

Behold, the very Word of God. It was there all along. I lied to you when I said you would not find the Word in your religion. But all you could hear then were lies. Only now, after this long journey, are you able to know the truth.

we can talk at starbucks

My oldest daughter doesn't believe in God anymore, so she says. She told me this recently at Starbucks.

Starbucks is the place we go to talk. The house is the place where we do the daddy/daughter thing. I enforce tough boundaries, which is my job, and she pushes hard against them, which is hers. Sometimes we argue passionately about this, which can be a strain. But when I take her to Starbucks, we become two different people. We sit down and she starts talking. She talks to me about everything at Starbucks.

So I like taking her to Starbucks, as you can imagine. It's our thing and we both know it. I'll say, "Let's go to Starbucks," and she'll give me the thumbs up. It means "Let's talk."

We were sipping our hot drinks and I said, "So tell me how you and God are doing these days."

She got a sad look in her eyes before she spoke. She never hesitated, apparently never even considered hiding this from me. She put a mock-frown on her face, which is a way of indicating that you are serious about what you are going to say. Then she shook her head slowly back and forth in the way people do when they want you to know they regret having to say something, but they must.

"Don't believe in him. I want to. I really wish I did. I've tried to believe in him, but I just don't."

I'd say about a hundred thoughts rushed into my head in that instant. But the thing that pushed its way to the surface was a warning thought. "Be very careful with her. Listen to her. Don't speak."

How and what we humans think about God is usually enmeshed with what is going on in our lives at any particular time. God language is deeply rooted in our psyche and perhaps our collective unconscious, if you believe in that sort of thing. I'm not sure I do, but it seems to explain a lot. That's why even those who do not believe in a deity might still yell, "Jesus Christ!" or "Oh my God!" in a moment of anger, passion, or fear. The language of God is deep and old and practically inescapable for most people.

When someone is giving you their theology, their God words, you should listen hard and be very gentle. The time to deliver your God words is when you are asked.

You see, I'm on this journey that she is beginning. This God stuff is my specialty, you might say. Like if a brick layer's son was talking about building his first wall. And if I'm not careful, I'll rush in with my answers and my story. If I'm not careful I will overwhelm her with my own journey.

And this is her journey. I will willingly and passionately share my own journey with her, when the time is right. God, help me with the timing on this. She needs enough of me and not too much.

So she talked and talked and talked. She cried and so did I. As I listened, two things grabbed my attention.

First, it's her inability to feel God's presence that is making it hard for her to believe. She said, "I don't really care that I can't see God. I've already figured out that our senses mislead us. There are a lot of real things in the universe that we cannot see or touch or understand. I don't really need to see or touch God to think that God might exist. But I don't feel God inside. Things don't seem real to me unless I can feel them."

I made a mental note to follow up on that, because I don't really understand it. It sounds like her mother. I, on the other hand, coming out of a lot of experiences with emotional religion, don't trust my feelings. I always needed to understand the idea of God. That's what I was always looking for in the old days.

Second, she loves church. She said she really likes our church and certainly doesn't want to stop coming. She said she likes my sermons and that they really make her think.

I started crying again when she said that. Just a little. Watery eyes.

And so she will continue to be active in our church. She's keeping her eyes and her heart open. She would like very much to believe in God and hopes that God might make himself or herself feel real to her someday. Maybe sometime very soon.

I was so happy to hear that she loves church. It seems to me that she stands in a place that is exactly the opposite of many people in our culture. I meet people all the time who believe in the existence of God, but who are so wounded by their experiences with church that they drop out of the practice of Christianity because they see nothing but hurtful and abusive behavior in it.

This is my daughter, my baby girl, who is growing up and thinking and experiencing and searching. This is my daughter who is passionate and engaged and searching. This is my daughter.

And my daughter doesn't believe in God.

She sat in my lap and let me read baby Bible stories to her when she was very little. She sat on the blanket with the children of our church when she was a child. She gave her life to Christ in Vacation Bible School one year. She has grown up in the company of gentle people of faith.

My daughter doesn't believe in God right now. Why do I feel so happy?

Because she wasn't afraid to tell me.

Because the roots of faith that we have given her were born of a gentle and authentic Christianity. I trust that she will find her way in time, and further, that all of this will be her journey and her story. It will all be good.

Because I love her mind and her passion. You should see her. She talks about God more now that she doesn't believe in God than ever before. She goes around her high school asking people what they think about God. She told me that if a boy can't tell her what he thinks about God, she's not interested in him. She's looking for a boy who is a deep thinker.

And because she and I can go to Starbucks and talk. How she honors me with this. Can she possibly know what that means to me, that she wants to talk to her father?

I don't suppose she will until the day that she sits with a son or daughter of her own and asks, "So how are you and God doing these days?"

big numbers and little girls

I'm in my office reading *Billions and Billions* by Carl Sagan and glancing occasionally at the picture of my youngest daughter that is on the screen of my computer.

In this very moment, right now, I am being pulled in opposite directions by two distinct and powerful forces in my life. The one is my desire for truth and my commitment to be fearless and unashamed in my search for it. The other is my joyful adoration of the smallest and most precious things in the world.

I delight in a chipped marble I once found on a remote part of our church property, a marble that must have lain there for half a century or more. Once I nearly swooned at the sight of a little girl wobbling on her first bicycle with a soiled Band-Aid attached only at one end and flying like a flag from her skinned knee. This is one way that I look at the world.

I also look at the world with a stubborn determination to keep my eyes open and to trust the evidence before me. Mindless forces tear at our planet with apparently no regard for life, liberty, or the pursuit of anything. Nature cares not for suffering. Lions sometimes kill baby elephants over agonizing hours by eating them from their hindquarters up. Their cold, emotionless eyes reveal a consciousness incapable of concern for the screaming agony of their prey. The night sky, likewise, is more than the simple dome that Genesis describes. It is, in fact, the glass through which we gaze with infant eyes at a universe which is beautiful, but completely beyond us. The unknown forces that create the stars seem random and are violent beyond anything we can imagine.

So you see, this moment I am sharing with Sagan and Lillian is not the first time my life has been pulled in different directions by adoration and reality.

Carl Sagan is the one who got us thinking about billions back in a day when millions meant something to most people. Sagan touched our provincial eyes and bade us see. And see we did. He provided the first glimpse of the universe to a generation who watched Cosmos on TV. For many of us, that was the first time we realized how small we really are. We are so small as to be unable to imagine the size of our own tiny planet. The size of our solar system is utterly beyond all comprehension. Voyager 1, the fastest space vehicle ever created, has only recently left our solar system after thirty years of travel. At its present speed, it would take about 80,000 years to reach the Alpha Centauri system, our closest star neighbor in this spiral arm of the Milky Way Galaxy.

Really, why even talk about the size of the universe? That conversation involves numbers that only make sense to mathematicians and astronomers who are fluent in the language of exponentials. With our measly millions and billions, what business do you and I have in speaking about the universe?

So here I am, reading Sagan and looking at Lillian, and I am now remembering Annie Dillard's book *For the Time Being*. Dillard rightly notices that much of what we see and experience in the world leads us to think that the individual does not matter. The horrific brutality and utility of natural selection scoffs at our sentimental love of individuals. Even individual species mean nothing to the blind forces of evolution.

And looking to the heavens does not give us comfort if we are searching for our worthiness there. Even now galaxies are colliding, obliterating solar systems as they slowly grind through each other. What would you say if I told you that an entire planet was destroyed on the other side of the universe, wiping out an entire race of intelligent beings? They are gone, along with their history, their art, their philosophy, and their desperate spiritual longing for God.

You would say, "That's a shame."

What would they say if they heard the same about us?

A tsunami rocks the ocean bottom sending a locomotive wave to slap at our matchstick villages. Sophisticated theologians say there was no Godly anger or vengeance behind those waves. Does it make them feel better to think that the waves were random furies of nature? Is it a comfort to think of our world as a cold and mindless orb where tectonic plates grind together, greased with the bodies of those unfortunate enough to live above their tortured seams?

And in the middle of these thoughts, I cast my eyes upon the picture of my youngest daughter, her hands clasped together, her eyes gleaming and intelligent behind the smallest glasses you have ever seen. This is Lillian Hope Atkinson, named in honor of Jesus who once said, "Consider the Lilies of the field." This is Lillian, whose precious eyes twice moved me to write about her bifocals. This is Lillian. She is just one of billions and billions of children born on this planet in the years since Homo sapiens first walked its surface. There is no rational argument that can be made to support the idea that she is in any way special or of any importance in the Cosmos. Neither her life or her death, her suffering or her joy will move the planets or influence the stars.

And yet she lives at the center of the universe of my mind and heart. Were she to die tonight her death would be but a tiny ripple on the surface of the vast ocean of reality, but I would be wounded unto death. I say unto death because you never recover from the death of your child. My wife once met an elderly woman in the hospital. In the middle of their conversation, the woman was overcome by racking sobs. She was crying for a baby who died as an infant, some sixty years before. Her grief was still that raw.

And so I look at Sagan's book and Lillian's picture. Suddenly I want to bow my head and curve my shoulders, putting my arms around her and drawing her into the tabernacle of safety under my chin. I would turn my back on the Cosmos and whisper into her ear, "Don't listen to it. You are special. You are unique. You are Lillian."

Somehow the same mind that shows me the bleak realities of the universe also tells me that there has been no child born of man who is like unto Lillian. She is unique in all of history and in all the universe. And this too is a truth that must be reckoned with.

Our common humanity cannot, will not abide the thought that a child does not matter. With one eye on the sky and the other suspiciously watching the movement of the earth, nonetheless we stake our claim.

We are unique. We are important. We matter. And our best impulses lead us to cherish and celebrate these truths. Some of us cradle what is beautiful and good, pushing it through the filters of our creativity. They are artists. Some of us rush across the face of creation to rescue people in pain or in need. They are saints. Some of us work for goodness in quiet ways and in little towns. They are heroes.

On Sunday mornings, when I arrive at the church before the breaking of dawn, I am mindful that I join myself with the communion of saints across the years in singing ritual songs of human worth and of God's interest and care. I like to think of Christianity, with its stunning and impossible story of the ultimate worth of humanity, as an offering to what we feel in our bones must be true.

If our ultimate worth cannot be seen or divined from the rocks and the stars, we will hold hands across the face of the earth and sing it into existence. If it seems at times that God cannot be found, there are millions of people across the face of the earth demanding God's existence. This means something. We demand value for ourselves and for each other. God language – theology – speaks of that value in ways that are inclusive of everyone. God words are archetypal. People can hear God words.

There is something deep and uncompromising within us that cannot look upon the face of a child and consider her to be merely fodder for evolution's hard turning. And even though we often sin by not living in ways that reflect the values we feel, when we remember our sin we feel ashamed and dehumanized and repentant. We wish we were better people.

This is another major theme of the Christian spiritual path. We aren't the people we want to be. We admit this, like alcoholics, and gather together to walk with the Spirit of God, one day at a time. After many years, we find that our souls have been changed for good. We hope and pray that we live in ways that reflect what we dream and hope for humanity.

I stand behind Lillian with my hands on her shoulders. We look into the night sky, and I show her once again the belt of Orion, hanging there near the band of stars that is our only view of the Milky Way. I stand with Lillian, and BY GOD I will see goodness and mercy in the stars and in ourselves.

And I will stand in peace and with love beside all others who see the same.

the seventh sister

What will it be like when you are gone, I wonder? You've been with us for so long. It's hard to remember what it was like before you came.

First there was a line between two points, a single dimension. It was like living before consciousness. There was no awareness of others. No need for it. It was just the two of us, and I was happy with things the way they were.

Then you came into our world and added a new dimension. You turned a line into a triangle with three sharp points. Everything changed, and I was afraid at first. But then you became my little buddy. Believe it. I took you everywhere in those days. I carried you high on my shoulders, behind my head. Your legs dangled in front of my chest, and I held your ankles in my hands. I wanted to show you everything—the whole world.

When the news came that we were becoming a square, I felt jealous and protective. I didn't want a newcomer to ruin our triangle. A part of me knew that there would never again be one little girl who was my buddy. But she came, and we saw that she was also good. In time we settled into a four-cornered life.

Then a third girl came, and we took on the shape of a star. In time I came to love our star-shaped family. I even made my own private constellation. I renamed the belt of Orion and began to call it The Three Sisters in honor of my little girls.

Years passed. Each November The Three Sisters rose in the night sky. I watched them and smiled. Things changed. You grew older and wiser and more interesting to me. And I got older too. My shoulders can no longer hold you, and the view is not enough for you anymore.

You were the rooster, the one who announced a new day and a new era. The end of our line and the beginning of our shapes. Reiley Rooster Simon and Schuster. I swear we used to call you that. And oh how you did fly from animals to books, from Old McDonald to Jung, from little girl to young woman.

So what are you saying? Are you saying that we're going back to being a square again? Are you telling me that you're going away, and you're not coming back?

Never? Only for visits? Are you serious?

I knew this day would come, but I never let myself think about it. Never until now at the very end.

Okay, you growing up and having your own life is a good thing. I know that. But before you go, I want you to look into the night sky. Look past our beloved Orion, far above his shoulders and even beyond the red eye of Taurus that sees all. There in the blackness you will see a little teacup constellation of six stars. Many ancient people called it The Seven Sisters.

There were seven stars in this constellation once, thousands of years ago. Seven sisters, but one of them disappeared. One day someone counted, and she wasn't there anymore. No one knows where she went. Who knows how something like that happens. Maybe it was just her time. Time for that little star to go her own way. And yet, for centuries, they were still known as The Seven Sisters. The seventh sister went away, but I like the idea that they kept the name and maybe a place for her at the table, just in case she came home for a visit.

Somewhere along the way a modern person said, "Hey, there are only six stars." And now people usually call them the Pleiades, which is the Greek name for The Seven Sisters. But I guess it doesn't draw attention to the fact that one of them has gone her own way.

I'll tell you what I'm going to do. In honor of you, our departing sister, I officially reject the name Pleiades. I'm going back to the old name. As far as I'm concerned, that little teacup above Orion is called The Seven Sisters.

Can I rename the stars whenever I like? Don't ask me; you know I can.

So now it is your time. I know that. I see you chomping at the bit, ready to take your life into your own hands. This change is right and good, but it hurts more than I ever imagined. Because no matter how often people say, "Oh, she'll come home sometimes," and "She'll always be your daughter," you and I know that things will never be the same. My little buddy is leaving, and she doesn't fit on my shoulders anymore. That's the truth, and I resent anyone who suggests that it shouldn't hurt like hell.

So go now, while I am being foolish and philosophical. Now is the time. Go, my strong young woman. Go right up in the face of life. Seize everything. Do not back down or back away.

Sit high above the shoulders of Orion; I want you to see everything.